T0121097

Broken
in All
the Right
Places

Healing in His Hands

PAMELA SALETRI PARRON

WESTBOW
P R E S S®
A DIVISION OF THOMAS NELSON
& ZONDERVAN

WestBow Press books may be ordered through booksellers or by contacting:

WestBow Press
A Division of Thomas Nelson & Zondervan
1663 Liberty Drive
Bloomington, IN 47403
www.westbowpress.com
844-714-3454

Because of the dynamic nature of the Internet, any web addresses or
links contained in this book may have changed since publication and
may no longer be valid. The views expressed in this work are solely those
of the author and do not necessarily reflect the views of the publisher,
and the publisher hereby disclaims any responsibility for them.

Any people depicted in stock imagery provided by Getty Images are
models, and such images are being used for illustrative purposes only.
Certain stock imagery © Getty Images.

Scripture quotations marked (AMP) are taken from the Amplified
Bible, Copyright © 1954, 1958, 1962, 1964, 1965, 1987 by
The Lockman Foundation. Used by permission.

Scripture quotations marked (NIV) are taken from the Holy Bible, New
International Version®, NIV®. Copyright © 1973, 1978, 1984, 2011 by Biblica,
Inc.® Used by permission of Zondervan. All rights reserved worldwide. www.
zondervan.com The "NIV" and "New International Version" are trademarks
registered in the United States Patent and Trademark Office by Biblica, Inc.®

Scripture marked (KJV) taken from the King James Version of the Bible.

Scripture quotations marked (TLB) are taken from The Living Bible copyright
© 1971. Used by permission of Tyndale House Publishers, a Division of
Tyndale House Ministries, Carol Stream, Illinois 60188. All rights reserved.

ISBN: 978-1-6642-2385-1 (sc)
ISBN: 978-1-6642-2386-8 (hc)
ISBN: 978-1-6642-2387-5 (e)

Library of Congress Control Number: 2021903319

Print information available on the last page.

WestBow Press rev. date: 07/01/2021

I dedicate this book to Jobanna Salsman, whose faithful love and encouragement lifted my face to fix my eyes Jesus and reminded me whose I was in a season of discouragement. But she didn't stop there; she saw this book in me and pulled it out, gently prodding and stirring me "up to love and good works" and breaking down my excuses and bad habits.

Jo, without your patience and faithfulness, I would not have finished this book. Because of your godly influence and friendship, I have a renewed purpose.

Jo, I love you, miss you, and look forward to seeing you again in heaven and thanking God in all my remembrance of you.

CONTENTS

ACKNOWLEDGMENTS AND THANKS

This book examines the foundations of my faith, an ongoing process, but my fierce battles during my young adulthood were essential and yet so painful to revisit. There is no way I could have done this without the faithful prayers and encouragement of the Sisters Loved by God, a women's Bible study group. Love and prayers to all of you.

Thank you, Jo, for without your influence and encouragement, there would have never been a Sisters Loved by God or this book.

Thank you, Sherrie and Cheryl, for the hours of work revising my written words, and for listening, encouraging, and praying with me, in addition to your gift of friendship. I am so grateful.

To my mom and dad for teaching me the Bible and songs, and dragging me to church, prayer meetings, and Awana, an evangelical ministry for kids with special emphasis on Bible memorization. You planted God's Word in my heart. For your love and support always, thank you! I love you.

Eric, we've shared a lifetime; you have always been there to provoke me and argue, but little brother, you have pushed me to speak precisely and clarify my strong feelings with concise words—despite your almost always being on my side. I love you!

From my earliest memories to today, my life has been enriched by so many people God used to shape and develop me, and I am so grateful today for all of them. I had to pull out pictures I hadn't looked at in years, and the Lord smiled as I remembered you with renewed gratitude.

Joel and Michelle, I'm so thankful that God entrusted you to us. You are treasured! You have taught me so much without knowing it.

To my husband, Antonio. You have faithfully loved me as Christ has for decades. Thank you for your patience; you have held my hand and my heart through laughter and tears. You are my one true love.

PREFACE

I want you to understand a few things before we continue. For years, people suggested that I write this book, and I tried a few times but without success. My computer in the corner of the room was a permanent reminder of this looming sense of duty to write it, but I just couldn't get it out. I could invite you over for coffee and tell you anything you wanted to know (within the realm of my knowledge and experience—no math questions please). Speaking comes easily to me while writing rips my insides apart when I stir up memories that have been so carefully packed away.

Writing is a solitary action. I can't gauge what I'm saying to you or focus on what your interests are or what I think would help you based on your reactions. It's left to me to figure out what to say that might encourage you. Instead of unpacking a part, I took out the whole thing to look over and decide what should go where and how and what should be put away again. The pain and despair can be overwhelming because there is a lot of that in my memory. Hearing those discouraging whispers again made me grab my box of Kleenex and leave the writing undone.

What could I say to encourage others when I still got emotionally messy in the quiet of my thoughts? How about integrity? Now I'm coming to the heart of what I desperately want you to understand for your sake and mine. I need to be free from the fear of your misunderstanding that I am someone I am not. I still struggle with questions and nagging doubts, daily physical pain, and the irritations of daily life. I still fail, fall short of expectations, and sin. So who am I to tell you anything? Nobody. That was my main problem with writing this book.

"So why are you writing this book?" you ask. It's because God has confirmed to me on several occasions that He wants me to write this to encourage people who hurt, are in despair, and doubt that there is a good God in heaven. I don't have all the answers, nor do I feel worthy of writing, but God says that His grace is enough for me.

> For it is by free grace (God's unmerited favor) that you are saved (delivered from judgment and made partakers of Christ's salvation) through [your] faith. And this [salvation] is not of yourselves [of your own doing, it came not through your own striving], but it is the gift of God; Not because of works [not the fulfillment of the Law's demands], lest any man should boast. [It is not the result of what anyone can possibly do, so no one can pride himself in it or take glory to himself.] For we are God's [own] handiwork (His workmanship), recreated in Christ Jesus, [born anew] that we may do those good works which God predestined (planned beforehand) for us [taking paths which He prepared ahead of time], that we should walk in them [living the good life which He prearranged and made ready for us to live]. (Ephesians 2:8–10 AMP)

I learned these verses as a child, but it has taken me a long time to really digest their meaning, which is why the Amplified version best explains what I'm trying to say. I always thought I'd arrive at a degree of maturity where I could be ready and worthy of doing something in service to God, but I will never measure up physically, emotionally, mentally, or spiritually. I will continue to depend on God to complete me to do the things that He planned for me to do.

I am loved, rescued, redeemed, forgiven, accepted, strengthened, and empowered by God's grace through faith in Christ Jesus and by the indwelling of the Holy Spirit. You can be too if you have faith in God by belief in Jesus.

God never intended for us to do things for Him apart from Him. He has done everything for us and asks us to take Him at His Word, to trust Him so that we can live life abundantly in His presence. It is my daily decision to obey His leading instead of my leading Him to some good project I've chosen and asking Him to bless me in doing it. That should be easy, but there has been a fight for the allegiance of my soul.

For years, I have believed in God, and for years, He has shown me what that means. He has repeatedly asked me to trust Him; I have answered that request in many ways but have eventually said yes with a clenched jaw, drenched pillows, joyful exuberance, reluctant resignation, and perfect peace—not necessarily in that order. Still, He whispers, "Trust me." I see His presence everywhere. His faithfulness brings me to my knees; it has given me the courage to sit at this desk, unpack the stuff of my life, and return to writing again.

Many people have challenged, comforted, and encouraged me. I have tried to be an island, an imaginary princess locked in her tower and so on with withering results. But those of us who believe in Jesus Christ, "the called-out ones," the church, are compared to a body made up of many connected parts (1 Corinthians 12). I have been blessed with the encouragement and support all the way along whenever I was willing to embrace it. God has powerfully used all kinds of people in my life whom our modern pragmatic society might have even looked down on or dismissed. God likes to surprise us that way.

I have been actively involved in a women's Bible study group whose love and prayers are a huge reason I could return to this task. Through reading, I connected with people from centuries past and contemporaries I have never spoken to, and I have been encouraged by their words and testimonies. So I write with the hope-filled prayer that you will be encouraged to keep looking for God and

lean on, trust in, and be confident in the Lord with all your heart and mind and do not rely on your own insight or understanding. In all your ways know, recognize, and acknowledge Him, and He will direct and make straight and plain your paths. (Proverbs 3:5–6 AMP)

CHAPTER 1

Life Is Unfair

❧

I vividly recall my last steps. My feet moved slowly along a narrow concrete path leading from our front door to the sidewalk illuminated by a streetlight on that chilly early summer morning. I had a feeling of something being wrong without the anxiety that usually accompanied it. Leaning on the arm of my fiancé, I heard only our shoes scraping on the pavement as we moved toward the family van waiting to drive me to the emergency room. During the twenty-minute drive, I watched the blackened silhouettes of the rural Wisconsin countryside passing by as I felt myself slipping away.

After that, my memory fades in and out. Troubled faces of those I loved looking on helplessly. Placed in a wheelchair and wheeled from the van to the receptionist's desk. Lifted onto a hospital bed while our family doctor kept saying my name with his distinctive Indian accent. His usual relaxed and cheerful nature was abruptly replaced with impatience and seriousness. The concerned voices of the nurses and my doctor quickly turned to alarm and urgency. As they feverishly worked around me, they became a blurred backdrop. "No blood pressure" and "slowing pulse" are some words I remember hearing. The repeated attempts to start an IV captured my last bit of attention and anxiety. I recall something about putting a needle to my heart as my consciousness flickered out; I was dying.

I had lived a good life. I had experienced many aspects of life. I had known all kinds of people and places. In many ways, I had lived more in eighteen years than some had during a longer time. The last years had been a life lived to the fullest. I was full of expectations and idealism as I started down the path of discovering and defining who I would become and what I would do with my future. I guess I was much like most people my age—indignant that the world was not what I had hoped for and wishing I felt more grown up and in control. It seemed at that moment on August 13, 1988, just short of my nineteenth birthday, that I was as grown up as I would ever be.

My young dying body was in the hands of the helicopter medical evacuation team who took me from rural Wisconsin to the university hospital in Madison. It was a three-hour trip by car; I have no idea how long it took in the helicopter. I have no memory of any of it. I had lost consciousness much earlier. I can only imagine the faces of my fiancé and my parents as that helicopter took off. They had been told to hope and pray for the best but to expect the worst.

All that schooling and homework, papers, and especially math for nothing! Life is so unfair! So is death. Obviously—not to break the suspense—I lived, but how many times in the following days, weeks, months, and years did I wish this life had ended … A tragic end? Perhaps. But it would have been an end on a high note. Looking back, I think it made for a good romantic tragedy of a young Christian girl trying to sort out her circumstances and her relationships with God and those around her. Just as happily ever after was finally in sight, but before it could be spoken or more realistically messed up, it would just read, The End.

In the beginning of this story, two lost people found each other, fell in love, married, and started a family. My mom had lost her way in her faith before she met my dad, but by the time I was born, she was back in church and praying for my dad. We had moved four times and added a little brother before we settled down in Denver.

Dad worked for the government, which is why we moved around. It was there that my father, a former self-proclaimed atheist, accepted Jesus as his Savior and decided to go to seminary. He loves to study things, so he went to seminary more to study about God out of a love for knowledge than out of a calling to ministry. He didn't want to trust the commentaries alone to understand the Bible. The logical next step for him was to learn Hebrew and Greek, the original languages of the scriptures. He committed his life to Christ when I was a toddler. During the first years after his conversion, church friends became our extended family. I asked Jesus into my heart when I was four and was baptized when I was seven. Since I was not yet able to touch the bottom of the baptistery at that age, I kicked the pastor trying to remain upright.

A car accident changed our lives. We had been on a lonely highway at night when a drunk driver crossed over the middle patch of earth that separated one direction from the other and hit our car head on at fifty-five miles per hour. I had been thrown headfirst into the windshield of our car since I had not had a seat belt on at the time. I started my first day of kindergarten looking like a mini Frankenstein. I had a reverse Mohawk, and that shaved middle section was lined with ten widely spaced stitches from the front of my head to the back. It did not help me socially adapt to school. My father's fractured vertebrae were fused, but the pain caused his desk job to be unbearable.

I still picture my father lying over a lime-green beanbag poring over Greek and Hebrew translations of the Bible. My mom's knees had been injured, and her whole body had been affected by the damaging jolt. My brother had a slight scrape and a small cut between two toes, which remains a mystery to this day.

Eventually, my father had to relinquish his government job due to his disability. He stepped down and decided to accept a higher calling. Sooner or later, God calls us all to ministry in one way or another. My father had been actively involved in church, but he had told God he would never be a pastor. Never give God ultimatums. I officially became a PK (preacher's kid) at age nine.

We moved from a Denver suburb next to the majestic Rocky Mountains down to the hot, dry desert. The stark mountains surrounding the valley of the sun seemed like a Mars landscape that was specifically designed to trap the oven-like air in the Phoenix metro area. Dad's calling brought our family to this strange new place and a much smaller one-story house.

Another dramatic change occurred in our schooling. We had attended a strict private Christian school in Denver. In Arizona, my little brother and I went to the public school behind our house. My mother had always been at home; however, with the loss of income, she started working at Sears. In Colorado, we had attended a church with a lot of families that were like mine; the first day of church in Arizona was our family of four and an older retired couple in a small church in a rural area about eight miles from home.

At nine, my life had dramatically changed, and I felt sorry for myself. I made some friends, but I never felt that I fit in. I wore odd clothes, or so said my classmates, which were what we could afford. Far worse, I was a big girl for my age, which might have been all right had I been coordinated. I couldn't be cute, and though I tried, I wasn't good at sports. I looked in the mirror and saw big and ugly staring back.

I never felt I measured up. I babysat, I sang, I memorized Bible verses, I played musical instruments, I got straight As, and I was the teacher's pet though I didn't look up when I knew the answers because I didn't want to invite my classmates' scorn.

I played soccer, roller-skated, and swam and swam and swam, but I was never good enough in my mind; I grew to hate myself. Summers were my refuge because my family took long road trips camping all over the US; my brother and I still tell stories about those trips. But they all ended too soon.

In sixth grade, I was sure God delighted in punishing me. I seriously planned on running away for a while to the abandoned parsonage next to the country church so everyone would miss me, try to understand how badly I hurt inside, listen to me, and feel sorry for not appreciating me. I thought about it enough to realize that it maybe would prove to be dangerous and painful, and so I decided I just wanted to die as if that would be less painful or dangerous.

I can still picture this eleven-year-old girl alone under a mulberry tree in the playground after another round of taunting with her fists raised to heaven saying, "God, I hate you! You're so unfair!" The bitter tears were washed away as I swam in our backyard pool, but my hatred grew as I swam in a pool of self-pity. How could God say He loved me when I was so miserable? Even so, I prayed, I sang in church, and I set the best example could. I listened to my father's teaching at church and at home. I listened to my mom and the preachers on the radio. Meanwhile at school, I even tried to lie to get my peers to respect me, but they didn't. The result? I hated myself even more. I hated school intensely.

For the first time since I had started at my new school, I had subject matter that I didn't already know. My first two years in school in Arizona had been mostly a review of what I had learned at the private school in Colorado. I had to concentrate and learn, but I felt I did not care to anymore. Straight Fs brought my parents to school, and at home, my conversation let the contempt I had for myself and this world seep out. With my parents' full attention, the floodgates burst with the waters of bitterness I had so carefully gathered in my soul. They were dismayed, confused, and saddened by this child who had been so deeply pierced with such negative thoughts. They spoke of my beauty, talents, and ability as well as God's love, plans, and purposes. Dad made a card for me with a stop sign on one side and Philippians 4:8 (NIV) on the other.

> Finally, brothers, whatever is true, whatever is noble, whatever is right, whatever is pure, whatever is lovely, whatever is admirable—if anything is excellent or praiseworthy—think about such things.

I asked my parents for forgiveness; I did not wish to embarrass or disappoint them again. I tried more or less to continue at school.

5

I tried to blend in resigned to the idea that I was a loser. My parents' encouraging words were in my mind betrayed by the cold realities outside my home.

A new opportunity to start over came that summer. Most of my parents' families resided in Wisconsin, and for various reasons, we moved there. During the summer, we spent a lot of time at my grandparents' nine-hole golf course and different aunt and uncles' dairy farms. For the most part, it was a welcome change that offered many opportunities for me to be useful and to daydream. I especially loved being with my cousins on my great aunt and uncle's dairy farm, where I had barn clothes and boots and was expected to wake up and do chores with everybody else. I think that was the only time in my life that waking up early was OK.

We played great games, prepared for the fair, and had so much fun. It was an island of joy in my moat of misery. Through God's grace, my aunt and uncle "adopted" another moody teenager in an already full house. That summer passed all too quickly, and yet our family still didn't have a permanent home.

While my father was speaking at different churches and prayerfully considering them as our possible home (and vice versa), we lived in Milwaukee with my dad's brother. Considering my emotional fragileness, the busing situation in the city, and our temporary living arrangements, my parents placed my younger brother and me in a small, private Christian school with a dress code. Girls wore dresses but not uniforms; our family's limited resources were used for tuition, not for wardrobes.

At that time, I was taller than most of the grown women I knew. My dresses were in the eyes of a seventh grader old lady hand-me-downs. I wanted so badly to be accepted in this new place. The first day of school, I walked in to see perfectly groomed young ladies in impeccably fashionable dresses. Being the tallest, I was seated in the back row where I could fully appraise my peers. The academic material was advanced, and my impulsive behavior reflected my lack of ladylike Christian training gained only in the hallways of such institutions. Ironically, it was this same training I had exhibited during my first days in public school in Arizona just a few years earlier that had set me at such odds with my peers in fourth grade. Once again, I was the odd one out except that time in a polite, proper, smiling, "You're not one of us" way. Rejection hurts.

I spent hours roller-skating or walking with my headphones on around the lake where my uncle's townhouse was. Under the grey autumn skies of the Midwest, I had questions. "Why, God did You have to make me like this? How can You say You love me when I hurt so badly and You do nothing?"

After a couple of months there, we moved to a home in a small town in the middle of the state. The distinguishing features of the town included no stoplights, one main street, and one elementary and one secondary school at opposite ends. I could ride my bike from one end to the other in five to ten minutes. The nearest McDonald's was a forty-five-minute drive away. We lived on the north end of Main Street right where the trucks started accelerating as they got out of town. We lived in an old parsonage, a house belonging to the church, about fifteen feet from the only Baptist church for miles.

When people who have lived in a place for only fifteen years are considered new to the area, you know you're in trouble. Everyone was friendly, but we were outsiders in a place where most residents had lived for generations. I tried my best to get along with everybody any way I could. Everybody knew who I was, and my parents knew everything I did before I got home from school. It was a small town. The church was small even by small-town church standards.

It was not a happy church in my mind; it was negative and critical. It didn't want change; it wanted to go back in time. The head deacon knew the Bible from cover to cover and sported frown lines as he quoted it. Ironically, I should have enjoyed this environment since I had a lot in common with them. Upon closer inspection and hindsight, I realize there were good, loving, supportive people there too, but I zeroed in on those whose qualities I most identified with. My brother and I were under constant scrutiny. Our family lived under a microscope. I tried again to measure up, find acceptance, and fit in.

Meanwhile, on the opposite side of the personality spectrum, my brother was not about to be forced to do anything against his will including smiling on the command of the deacons. My brother and I cringed and had our faith tested at church far more than anything we faced outside it.

I had become accustomed to being out of the inner sanctum of any circle of friends, but my desire to be accepted still oppressed me. Any time I was invited to do anything with anyone from school or church, I would do it thinking that maybe this signaled my initiation into that coveted place of acceptance. Compromise was probably the word that best characterized me. I became who I thought the present company wanted me to be. I was a Christian, but others' acceptance was my idol. I lived in conflict with who I was, who I wanted to be, and who I should be. Even worse, as a junior higher, the ideal of romantic love was in full bloom as well, and I was infected with its stench.

I was in no position to be a spiritual leader. I had a severe identity crisis and spiritual battle raging in my heart, mind, and soul. Standing in the void of a defined identity created by my lack of commitment in my personal faith, I stretched my hands to Christ to be the Lord of my life, that is, until the possibility of acceptance by my peers appeared to be attainable. The idea of belonging that I wanted so badly remained ever elusive.

After each episode, I was left empty and rejected, and that combined with the guilt of my sin against the One whom I knew had accepted me. I knew the truth, but I had not been set free because I was unwilling to give up this empty, elusive ideal of acceptance even knowing that it was a lie and it would never let me be free. It was the same lie that Eve believed so long ago; I wanted more.

However, I kept my internal struggle more or less tucked away. Everyone else saw the preacher's daughter who was five-nine and could have passed physically for a sixteen-year-old. This fact in addition to my chameleon-like ability to adapt at least temporarily to project an image I felt others expected or desired thrust an emotionally unstable almost thirteen-year-old into teaching and leadership at church and camp with all of the rough and raw edges of youth still there.

Thankfully, I do not remember all the details of my many failures. To everyone else, I was loud, opinionated, and wild with my attitude riding on an emotional teeter-totter of positive and negative with too little time up, too much time down, and only momentarily passing through the point of balance.

Never were these attitudes so prevalent as they were at Christian summer camp. I anticipated that first summer of Christian camp with great hopes of friendship and maybe more. After being in a church youth group of four, I was so ready to meet with Christian kids who were struggling in their faith just as I was. Finally, I'd have friends who would understand and accept me. I wanted to get away from the worldly games of love and friendship, right?

My junior high and high school looked better after I attended camp that first year. My schoolmates' behavior paled in comparison to the tactics employed in the struggle for dominance in the most popular and romantically successful Christian youth contest. Indignant anger and self- righteousness swelled and blistered in my heart. Those unrealistically high hopes were crushed as I found myself unworthy or not good or old enough to participate in that social environment. My first week of youth camp was painfully disappointing.

At the end of that week, I was asked/told (*volun*told) to serve as a camp counselor for the next two weeks of children's camps. In doing so, I discovered enough humility to call out and lift my hands in an I-give-up posture before God. I was a brokenhearted girl sitting on a log overlooking the lake, a place hidden from the rest of the camp, and pouring out her heart to God. I was praying that the pain of my selfish heart seeking its own glory and the embarrassment of my failures would go away. *Please, God—Change me.* The Holy Spirit interceded for me in ways I will know about some day in heaven. God gave me a good friend in that camp experience, another PK who struggled like me. I had been looking for the world's idea of good and almost missed the godly treasure of a good friend in another town. The following summer, I did not go to camp. Thanks to the generosity of family, friends, and our church, I went on a mission trip that continued God's work in me. I was thirteen and going to Europe. I was so excited. I wanted to get away and serve the Lord and meet whom I considered real Christians. I knew they would be real because we had to go through two weeks of boot camp with intense work, study, and preparation for ministry with no showers, no clothing changes, and no makeup. We would be living out of a tent and one bag all summer unless we were sleeping on the floor of a church or gymnasium. I didn't think having all those external props stripped away would be an attractive proposition for posers. I hoped for great spiritual growth and for the promise that I would go home changed because God knew I didn't like myself. I wanted change … and acceptance, and friends, and maybe more.

God allowed me to contract chickenpox after disobeying my mom; I thought she had exaggerated the infectious nature of this illness. I went to a friend's house for five minutes. My friend's mom took care of a couple of kids who had been sick with it. The kids weren't there when I stopped by, and of course I thought my mom was overreacting and being overly cautious when she said not to go over there. Besides, how could I say no to my friend?

As a result, a couple of weeks later, I went to meet my mission team, complete strangers, with a newly pockmarked face. My self-esteem was at a record low. I was feeling really ugly and still too tall; I have the pictures to prove it. God humbled and stretched me that summer. We stayed in England, Scotland, France, Italy, and Switzerland. It was great to have the privilege of seeing many places I had only read about, meeting amazing meeting people, and experiencing other cultures in the company of accepting, loving people who worked through any issues that came up between us.

Our English bus driver came to faith about a third of the way through our trip because he was so affected by what he saw and heard. It was the experience of a lifetime. I still did and said things I regretted, but I saw God work in the people around me and hoped and prayed He would work in me too.

I was changed at the end of that summer but not in the way I had wanted. I had hoped for this beautiful and perfect new me, but I was still the old me who struggled with my identity and did things I knew were wrong.

Three events affected me the most during that summer. First, at the end of the two-week boot camp, the director asked to have a meeting with all the preachers' and missionaries' kids. We had just ended a period of intense study, and I thought he would talk about our ministry in our families, a talk I had heard at other meetings in other places before. He didn't. He told us that we often got beat up by other people's expectations of us, but he said that we were special, and he gave us a special night out at a pizza place. This was a new concept—Being a preacher's kid was not a curse. We were special. I was special. This inspired my thought that just maybe God had placed me exactly where He wanted me. That thought would continue to challenge me for years.

Second, I had people besides my parents tell me that I was special. One of the leaders fixed my choppy short haircut and told me I was beautiful. I told myself that she was just being nice, but it was enough to make me think that maybe I was at least OK. My teammates listened and encouraged me. I messed up, and they forgave me. *Maybe I am OK*, I thought.

Third but most important, the night before we left for Europe, we held a consecration service with communion and foot washing. I had feet to match my height. They were big and ugly, too. I would never wear sandals without nylons. I preferred tennis shoes. When I realized what was going to happen, I panicked. There was no getting out of it. A candle on a table in the middle of our circle lit the room. The table also held the bread and juice. I knew I should be worshipping, but I was filled with dread; I was praying about me. I did not fear washing someone else's feet, but I did not want anyone to wash mine. Someone washed my feet as I fought back tears. When she finished, she hugged me and said, "God made you special and loves you and so do I." I felt God's presence there that night, and feeling released from dread and self-obsession, I worshipped God with the real though flawed Christians around me. God met us there that summer and blessed us.

That experience turned out to be a foreshadowing of things to come. I had to release my pride in a fantastical self-image where I tried to hide my flaws. I had to be humble enough to expose my big and ugly hurt and let God touch me where I needed healing and forgiveness. I had to expose my sin and shame without disguising or defending myself before I began to feel His presence. I could not see God when I was so obsessed with myself. Satan continually whispered, "Did God really …?" to perpetuate doubt about God's goodness and inflate my sense of self.

God did not demand my performance outside His perfection. God used flawed people, including me. God loved me, and that made me special. He loved me so much that while I still sinned, Jesus Christ came to die for me. In growing up, I had not experienced any huge tragedies, and yet I had managed to pick up so many big and ugly hurts. In pride, I wanted to prove I was worthy of being accepted. No, I was not worthy, but I was accepted through Jesus even with my big and ugly hurts, actions, attitudes, and all. I had become so focused on me and the baggage I had loaded on myself that I had become distracted from a simple truth that had made a four-year-old sing.

Jesus loves me this I know,
For the Bible tells me so.
Little ones to Him belong,
They are weak, but He is strong.

Yes, Jesus loves me.
Yes, Jesus loves me.
Yes, Jesus loves me!
The Bible tells me so.[1]

CHAPTER 2

Rinse, Repeat, and Spin

After an amazing summer, I was home again and ready to begin high school. Even in a small town, high school is a washing machine. There are many different colors some of which run. Some whites should be hand-washed individually. Some clothes are new while some are worn out. Some require hot water, special detergents, and bleach. But there's enough money for only one load in the industrial-sized washer that high school is. We throw everybody in there and hope for the best. Some clothes rise to the top while most are stuck in dirty water. There's no place to hide; everything affects everything else. When the timer buzzes, the ordeal is over, and everybody gets out. Some clothes come out fine while others have even bigger holes and are still dirty. That's how I felt about high school.

I would love to tell you that I had learned my lessons about my identity in Christ. I would love to say that I was a shining beacon of truth and light in my community and that my witness for Jesus stood tall and unmovable.

At church, I was criticized. At school, I wasn't that cool. It was not for a lack of trying though. I sang in the choir and was good at it. I played in the band, and we'll leave it at that. I played volleyball, took stats for basketball, and was the president of the drama and Spanish clubs. I was involved in everything I could be. (That's a good thing about a small school and church.) I still longed for an ideal of church, friendship, and love. I believe the only reason I made it out of high school relatively unscathed was that God protected me when I made unbelievably foolish and sometimes sinful decisions.

I struggled with depression because I never measured up to the expectations I had of myself. At times, I felt that a palpable darkness surrounded me. I tried to fight it myself, but I inevitably found myself on long walks talking to God and wishing I could grow up, wishing for others' acceptance, and wishing to feel loved. The irony and reality were that I did have friends, acceptance, and love. There are memories of sleepovers, camping, exploring adventures, swimming, horseback riding, canoeing, music, school games, and much more. There were also summer family vacations, besides the time spent on the golf course and farm. Some of the adventurous things we did make me laugh; others I wish I could go back and change.

Through it all, God gently called me. He used one of his gracious servants to minister to me. She lived in an assisted living center, used a walker, and lived on a missionary pension, which qualified her for government assistance. She gave me the most precious gift anyone could give—She prayed for me every day. My parents prayed for and with me every day, but that's what parents of faith are supposed to do. Miss Ruth came to church every time the doors opened and her health permitted it. She quietly and faithfully worshipped and prayed. She spoke softly and succinctly. I was sent on missions of mercy to make small deliveries.

I had sung and visited many nursing homes during my youth and thought it was good of me to visit her. I was so fixated on the criticism of mainly two older deacons that I almost missed the blessing God had for me. Miss Ruth had been a missionary to China and Malaysia for forty years; my father had asked her to pray over me before I left on my summer mission trip. My relationship with her grew as I looked into that frail face and saw bright blue eyes that danced with joy.

Slowly and only as requested, she shared her testimony with me. I always left with my mouth open. A missionary had visited her church when she was a girl and told the congregation that he knew God would call one of them to the mission field. She knew that call was for her. She knew she would probably never marry if she went to the mission field as a young woman even though she very much desired to be married.

Miss Ruth and I before I left on my summer mission trip, June 10, 1984

I went to her little apartment often to hear her stories of China when the Communists took over and her stories about her work in Malaysia. She never let me leave without praying with and for me. In her small apartment and in her presence, I began to see the shadow of God almighty around His faithful servant. I watched in wonder at Wednesday night Bible studies as this giant in the faith quietly listened to comments of others who arrogantly expounded on their beliefs of what the Bible taught. She was never recognized, never praised, never called on to share her experience or wisdom. *How can she sit there and take that? How can she be joyful? Why hadn't God blessed her with a husband or at least some respect in the church?*

I wondered. Her life's work could have easily been put into the volumes of books written about great missionary saints.

One time, my dad was asking the small Wednesday night group about putting our faith in God to work in the church and community. One deacon piped up as always to defend his inactivity in ministry opportunities because he was getting too old. Miss Ruth, in her late eighties, stood carefully holding on to the pew in front of her and walker beside her and quietly replied, "I know what you mean. I've had to cut my three Bible studies each week down to two." She sat gingerly. There was dead silence until my father started to laugh and praise her. I had never known that she led Bible studies with people who didn't attend our church. My father assured me later that serving God came as naturally as breathing to Miss Ruth; she didn't see such work as a ministry but as her "reasonable service" (Romans 12:1 KJV).

This dear woman did not mention her other work in the life of this spiritually confused pastor's daughter. We read the Bible together, and she answered all the questions I was too ashamed to ask anyone else. "How can you stand to go to our church?" I once asked her. She gently redirected me every time to look at God's face and seek His heart, not people's. It took years for her wise words to sink into my heart.

One day, I shared with her that a part of me was afraid to die because I hadn't really done anything for Christ. She replied, "I know how you feel. I feel the same way." I remember thinking, *I'm doomed. There's no hope for me.* So true. Hope is God's business. The psalms are filled with that assertion that there is hope in God alone (Psalms 25:5, 42:5, 11, 62:5).

This eighty-something woman influenced my life through her example and prayers in a way I will never fully know about until I reach heaven. Instead of analyzing my failures and inadequacies and looking down her nose at a floundering kid, Miss Ruth saw me as God did, and she knew I needed God's love and wisdom. I was blessed. On her wall was a poem-prayer I have since seen several times, and I always thanked God for her when I did. It basically said that many things may happen as a person grows older. Our bodies and minds may fail, but we should never forget that Jesus loves us. She never did. She didn't let the people around her forget either. Her precious Jesus welcomed her home a few years later, but the memory of her faith and love still encourages me on this side of heaven.

As a teenager, I had wanted to love God in a way that loving, serving, and praying for others would come as naturally as eating and breathing. The problem was my fixation on myself and what I considered good for me. My fixation on myself was prevalent when I was ready to graduate after three years of high school and move on. My parents were not about to send me to a state university at age sixteen. They supported sending me to a Christian college with a code of conduct, dress code, separate male and female dorms, a lock-in curfew at night, and noise and lights-out policies. I somehow still naïvely believed everything would be changed for the better after I left high school and that small church behind.

As my time to leave grew closer, I started to realize that I was also going to leave something much more precious—my little brother, taller than me, who had become perhaps my best friend, my encourager in the faith, and forever the devil's advocate to challenge my emotional declarations against his logic. We listened to our Christian music and leaned on each other when it seemed our parents had too much weight on them. I had been so eager to move on that I had not fully grasped the implications of being an eight-hour drive away and that life as I knew it would change.

Up to then, I had taken my parents and brother for granted. My expectations of them were unrealistic. My parents were not perfect, but they loved me and prayed for me faithfully knowing that only God could be my strength and protector. For the most part, they let me make decisions and handle the consequences. I never felt abandoned; they were there giving me instruction—too much if you had asked me. When I fell on my face, they helped me up and encouraged me but did not clean up the messes I had created. They were equally supportive of me in my successes and my failures. They assured me that failure was a part of living and that I should learn from it. They had repeatedly said that success and accomplishment were generally attributed to hard work and perseverance, and hard work did not kill me in spite of my protestations to the contrary. I learned that whining would not make the work go away or produce money; it would just make everyone around me irritated.

Being part of something meant I did my part at home, at school, at work, and at church. I learned that money takes longer to earn than to spend. My parents deliberately taught me not to judge people by their appearance or profession and to value everyone even when they smelled bad and used bad grammar or words. There were daily family devotions and prayers. Conversation, discussion, counseling, and best of all, laughter, happened most naturally around the dinner table. My parents' words were simply affirmations of the way they lived.

During my childhood and teen years when I felt spun around by the world at large, my own emotions, and distorted thinking, I learned that the more landmarks I used to center myself the better. My parents and brother stood tall and strong in my life despite my storms and theirs. Only after I left home did I gain an appreciation for the faith and stability of our home. I thought my family was how families were supposed to be; I didn't realize how fortunate I had been until later. Without my parents' unconditional love, strong faith, and consistent guidance, I would have destroyed myself. I had lived a blessed family life.

I should have known better than to put such high expectations on the Christian college I would be attending. I had changed schools five times alternating between public and private Christian schools growing up. Outside of the many rules of Christian schools including dress codes, people were still flawed, myself included. Somehow, I had wished that I would be a different, more mature person and that everyone around me would be improved too. I struggled alongside everyone else with sin Christian college or not.

I met many wonderful people at Grace College, and I had great respect for most of the professors; they were academically challenging and did not avoid discussing uncomfortable and controversial topics. I loved the opportunities to get off campus and be involved in other projects.

But that first semester, I was so disappointed that I hadn't found a Christian utopia that I began to question my faith. I used to sneak out the laundry room door, which was often overlooked and unlocked, to walk in the dark listening to my music. I would go to this bench behind a building by the lake, turn off the music, and cry my heart out to God. There was no reply. I started to question why I had held to certain values and if I was missing all the fun because of my devotion to God and my personal list of do's and don'ts. I rebelled. I tried living without restraint, but it was unfulfilling accompanied by a gnawing emptiness, which was frustrating. I stopped reading the Bible except for required classes and started going to the gym. Negativity consumed my good intentions; the desire for acceptance erased the lines I had drawn in the sand. A battle raged for control of my heart, mind, and strength. The angry voice of disillusionment urged me to abandon and become who knows what. An inaudible presence remained.

A long winter break was appealing, but financially, it made more sense for me to take an intensive course during that time, and astronomy seemed to be the best option for the science credits I needed to fulfill the requirements for my language-focused liberal arts degree. I was alone in my room most of the time, alone almost in the whole wing of the dorm. I had been ashamed at home, ashamed of my grades, my attitudes, myself. My lack of contentment gnawed at me. The longer I resisted praying and God in general, the emptier I became. God whispered in my solitude and silence.

Gazing at the winter constellations through my breath in the frozen winter sky made me vulnerable. As Abraham Lincoln stated, "I can see how it might be possible for a man to look down upon the earth and be an atheist, but I cannot conceive how he could look up into the heavens and say there is no God." Over the weekend,

I locked myself in my room pretending not to be there. I fasted, prayed, and worshipped. God broke through the barricade I had built around my hurting heart and once again touched me. "Come near to God and He will come near to you" (James 4:8 NIV). Thankfully, I never recovered from that meeting with God.

With renewed determination to live out my faith, I faced my second semester with new resolve and focus. One of my patient friends gave me a copy of an untitled essay by an anonymous author that I taped in a visible location to remind me to stay focused on God above all else. The relationship I had to pursue was the one with the Lord. Any human love relationship would be lacking unless the divine spaces were already filled with God's presence. Though it did not tell me anything I did not know, it became my tool to say out loud or read silently and then whisper, "God, I believe. Help me be satisfied with You alone."

God heard my prayers. Each of my friends touched my life probably more than they were ever aware. One of them arranged a job interview at a pizza restaurant where I could make more money than I was making working in the college cafeteria. I was only seventeen, and my friend's intervention and friendship were truly heaven-sent.

Even so, summer vacation looked bleak. Most people I knew were going home. I stayed near the college working in the cafeteria that provided meals for sports camps and conferences, and then at five o'clock, I started working at the pizza place until late. I rented a one-bedroom trailer with the friend of a friend and squeezed in as many summer school classes as I could between serving meals. I was extremely busy, but I had never felt so alone, unsure, and lost. I took many long walks by the lake in the early hours when I could not sleep. I prayed and cried to God about my future. I was so unsure what to do with myself.

I decided to complete my Spanish minor's overseas requirement by spending a semester in Madrid. A student I knew was going, so I wouldn't be going alone. I would not be able to work in Spain, so I worked as much as I could that summer. I did well enough at the restaurant to get a raise and even waitress. I was assured of a job upon my return at my current rate, which meant I could finally say goodbye to my job in the cafeteria after that summer was over. During that summer, I had an increasingly unquiet spirit that refused to be stilled. Late one night with just days to go until I went home for a visit before leaving for Spain, I took another walk to the lake. Winona Lake had ducks with no respect for man or vehicle; they were protected by law, and they knew it. One of the benefits of walking late at night was that they were sleeping and not underfoot.

Ducks aside, it was one of those nights when the pressure in my chest and the twisting of my insides were too unbearable for sleep. I went to my favorite bench hidden behind a building overlooking the lake. Hugging my knees to my chest, I again prayed, sang silently, and cried out to God. Everything was appropriately dark and silent. I saw muted grey shapes and heard occasional vehicles in the distance, but I concentrated on pulling out every stray thought and feeling to give to God. It passed timelessly until one question refused to be left without an answer: *What should I do with my life?* I knew that becoming a journalist at *National Geographic* was no longer the path I was to take especially with my grades. That being the case, I wondered if going abroad was necessary. There was no peace in my heart, and that time, I pressed for an answer. Whispering the names of every profession I had ever thought about in the darkness, I began to say those that recklessly jumped into my mind like *pastor's wife* though I had no idea how to prepare academically for that. Finally stumbling upon the words *Spanish teacher*, a duck quacked. There had been no other duck quacking that night. I prayed again because I had a strange but strong feeling that I had just been given an answer. *Lord, no kidding here—Should I study to be a Spanish teacher?* And I kid you not, that duck quacked again. God's comic relief at some of the most difficult moments in life is difficult to comprehend much less describe. All I know is that all the physical and emotional pressure left that moment, peace descended, and tears of joy ran down my face. Moses saw a burning bush; I heard a duck quack.

CHAPTER 3

Hope and a Future?

❧

I was going to Spain. Excitement blended with the pure terror of feelings of inadequacy and the unknown. Memories of my previous summer in Europe had proven to me that I did not need to pack a lot to survive. One object that I was leaving behind was my big, leather-bound Bible. I asked Dad for a paperback New International Version that we gave to visitors as it would fit easily in a big jacket or backpack pocket. I started reading *Let Me Be a Woman* by Elizabeth Elliot at a time when I was trying again to dedicate my life to God's will, trying again to be content with who I was and my circumstances instead of looking for greener grass or pining away for beauty, popularity, and romance.

I did not want to mess things up, but I was afraid I would. I read the foreword, which Valerie, Elliot's daughter, had written. The last paragraph contained the words I wanted to be my prayer. They were not my words or even Elliot's; they were the words of missionary Betty Scott Stam that Elliot had copied into her Bible and signed when she was ten or eleven.

Elliot was a revered woman of the faith, and these words represented what I wanted to say so precisely that I grabbed my pen as a new eighteen-year-old woman and wrote on the inside cover of that paperback Bible.

> Lord, I give up all my own plans and purposes, all
> my own desires and hopes, and accept Thy will for
> my life. I give myself, my life, my all utterly to Thee
> to be Thine forever. Fill me and seal me with Thy
> Holy Spirit. Use me as Thou wilt, send me where
> Thou wilt, work out Thy whole will in my life at any
> cost, now and forever.[2]

I signed my name before God in August 1987.

Time passed quickly; before I knew it, my family was driving to Chicago's O'Hare Airport. We left at 5:00 a.m. to arrive in time for my afternoon flight. Along the way, my parents made their expectations clear to me. We had had many missionary families stay in our home throughout the years, and I had heard many stories about cultural differences; some were humorous while others resulted in serious misunderstandings. We discussed these issues since I was given to pushing the envelope on everything. Dating was a clearly stated taboo. I grumbled that dating had never presented itself as an issue in my life before so I doubted it would be a problem. My parents warned me that new situations could overwhelm my sensibilities and that I was to be on my guard. I sincerely addressed their concerns and felt that I had left that subject to God. Admittedly, I had reserved the right to throw occasional pity parties. I adamantly said that I was fulfilling my course requirements—nothing more. Plus, this oversea experience was interrupting my job, which I needed. I was getting in, getting my coursework done, and moving out. Emphasizing every word, I boldly proclaimed that I would not become a missionary's or pastor's wife. I would serve God through my own work.

I was being honest. I had no burning desire to go to Spain; I would have gone to Mexico, Ecuador, Argentina, and so on had another student been going there. After thinking about it for about five minutes, I concluded that studying Spanish in Madrid sounded more illustrative on a resume and comparable to studying English at Oxford. There in three sentences lay the entire reasoning process behind my decision I'm ashamed to say.

On September 18, 1987, Sara and I boarded a plane that took us to a place that would alter the course of our lives. There was supposed to be another student with us, but she had canceled right before summer. Unfortunately, she had been the contact person with the missionaries we would be staying with until school began on September 27. We had no idea what the missionaries even looked like.

On our flight from New York to Madrid, we met a delightful elderly couple who spoke four languages. As we were arriving at Barajas International Airport in Madrid, we exchanged phone numbers and continued talking as we walked out of the terminal. We looked around but didn't see anyone. We exchanged some money so that we could call the number we had. No answer. I was in a panic, but at that moment, a few Japanese tourists walked up to Sara and in broken Spanish asked her how to use the phone. It was hilarious enough to bring a smile to my face. I turned as a woman with a kind face asked if I was one of the students from Grace College. I was so relieved that I think I hugged her.

That evening after a nap, we went out on the terrace of the missionaries' apartment. A young Spanish woman was staying at their apartment as well until she married three weeks from then. We were the only ones at home at the time because there was a meeting at church. We understood Patricia amazingly well despite a potential language barrier. She was friendly and honest. We sat there on the terrace watching the children playing and the neighbors talking and walking on the street below. I saw other people sitting on their terraces and enjoying the evening. A feeling of love and of coming home overwhelmed me. I began to wonder if I could extend my stay for the whole year. I was also aware that I was exhausted and that emotions could get the better me in that compromised state.

I sat silently in my thoughts as Sara and Patricia chatted. Sara's Spanish was much better than mine; my brain had become numb due to the effort of concentrating. Reason was trying to stop me as I was reeling head over heels in love with this little slice of Spanish life on the terrace. A tray of the biggest grapes I had ever seen was placed on the table next to me. Somehow, I conveyed that thought to Patricia, whose eyes sparkled as she said, "Quizás esta sea tu tierra prometida." "Maybe this is your promised land."

The next day was Sunday, and we attended Sunday school and church services. Before then, I had been unaware of the headaches that can develop from concentrating and processing a foreign language. Given that I had my paperback Bible and that the hymns were the same, I followed most of what was said, but it was hard work. Everyone greeted us with a kiss on both cheeks. I had to bend down for that because I was more than a head taller than most people there.

The missionaries gave us our orientation and even drove us to central Madrid, where we would eventually be staying. We helped them as much as we could around the church and their house. I was so grateful that we were with them, and I felt very much at home.

We met many people and tried to be useful whenever we could. We spent a day helping Patricia clean the apartment that would become her home when she married. I learned then that not all apartments were as nice as the one in which we would be staying. While that should have been obvious, it shocked me. A young man from the church who spoke some English became our friend and guide. Don't ask me how, but he ran into us when we were lost on more than one occasion and took us to our destination. Sara liked him right away.

On a trip in Madrid, Ricardo and Sara talked and talked and I walked behind them as I was having a private pity party about being the third wheel. Anyway, Ricardo had a friend named Antonio, who owned a car. They decided that the four of us should see a movie that we had seen in English. Sara informed me of this at the youth group meeting that evening. I was playing concentration with some younger kids who found me extremely entertaining due to my mistakes. (My concentration skills did not improve after that news flash. I later found bruises on my legs from smacking them so hard during the game.)

But the four of us driving around sounded like a date to me, something I had solemnly sworn would not happen. I was not Interested. However, to say no at that point would be offensive, right? I was going whether I liked it or not. And I did like it. They were perfect gentlemen though they got upset when they found we had left money in the back seat of the car when they dropped us off since they had not let us pay for anything. Remember, it was *not* a date.

The next day, we moved to our home with a Spanish family in Madrid. She was friendly, but we were tenants, so it did not feel like home. Thirty-two kilometers separated us from the missionaries, church, and everyone we had met. Alcalá de Henares was older than Madrid, famous for being home to the third oldest university in Europe and the birthplace of Miguel Cervantes, who wrote *Don Quixote*. Alcalá had felt like home while Madrid was a large capital city.

Sara and I started classes the next day. We used our transportation passes to get where we needed to go and to explore Madrid. There were buses, trains, and the metro, the subway system, which were all new to us Americans from the Midwest.

Sara and I visited the typical locations, but sometimes, we chose a destination just because its name sounded interesting. More than once, we got lost until we found the next metro stop to orient us. Our teachers, Ricardo, and Antonio were horrified when we told them one of our stories about where we had been, so we just stopped telling them about our adventures with the public transport system and walking and walking.

Everyone found out about our first major mishap though. We were going to arrive early before the Wednesday service to talk with Patricia. These trips were not covered by our transportation passes, so we had to buy bus tickets back to Alcalá de Henares. There were people in line when the familiar looking bus came, and we boarded. It took a turn we did not recognize, and slowly everyone got off the bus. We ended up in a city six or seven miles short of Alcalá. The bus driver was not helpful except to point in the direction of Alcalá and in the direction of the nearest bus station, where we would have to buy tickets to get there. We had passed that town on the bus before, but at that time, we did not realize the actual distance between the cities. We figured, "How far can it be?" So we decided to walk along the highway to get to Alcalá instead of trying to find a bus station that was who knew where in a city we did not know.

Fortunately, we arrived in Alcalá safe and sound although a little late for Wednesday service. Unfortunately, we were humiliated and blistered. Never again did we board one of those buses without double-checking its destination.

On the weekends, Ricardo and Antonio offered to take us home after services but only after we had gone out for coffee. I had never drunk coffee before coming to Spain, but I drank it to be socially acceptable, and I ended up liking it.

Initially, I had a problem with Antonio; I couldn't understand most of what he said. He had been born in Seville, in southern Spain, and he had a different enough accent that I couldn't catch what he was saying. Ricardo would repeat what Antonio had said or Sara would translate for me. I knew it frustrated him that I seemed to be able to understand everyone but him. Since he and I made up the leftover pair, I prayed to be able to understand him.

After three weeks of trying, I finally started to get it. Talking to people who knew him made my respect and admiration for him grow. There I was in forbidden territory—liking a guy who had the potential to be someone important in my life. I was excited, worried, and confused; the word *confused* appeared many times in my diary.

True to my nature, my favorite place became El Retiro, one of the major parks, one of the green lungs of Madrid; it was between our room and the school. I retreated there often to read, write, and pray. I quickly learned to look busy or inevitably someone would approach me to ask if I was American and then want to practice his or her English on me. I have always found it hard to say no to anyone, and more than once, I found myself in conversation with a stranger. At least I had the good sense to remain anonymous in public.

The people at school and in our house noticed we weren't taking advantage of Madrid's famous nightlife; we were in the minority of people our age. We didn't come to school on Monday mornings hungover. We were out and about, but we always returned bright eyed and happy. The lady of the house asked us where we went on the weekends. It opened the door for us to have several conversations with her and her family about our faith in God through Jesus.

I prayed fervently, read and memorized my Bible, and journaled my thoughts. I studied and practiced Spanish. I loved Spain. I realized that I was liking Antonio more and more every time we talked. His commitment to his faith in God was not so much talked about as it was evidenced in daily life and ministry. The common ground between us was the Bible and music; he played the guitar and sang. Everything else in our relationship grew out of that.

I desperately wanted to know what God wanted me to do in this situation. I read the prayer I had written in the front of my Bible many, many times: "I give up all my desires and hopes and accept Your will for my life." If I had met this guy at college and his name was Tony, I do not think I would have struggled so much. I did not want to lead him to think beyond a friendship if there was no future for us, but a life in Spain was appealing more and more to me not because I thought it was better than the United States but because I felt I could belong and be useful there. Oh the irony! I was a five-nine, blond, blue-eyed, jean-loving, English-speaking American. I stuck out like a sore thumb. But church was something I had taken for granted in the States, and in Spain, it was small and precious and in need of all its members' contributions. I felt I could contribute; maybe my life in Spain would make a difference, and that appealed to me.

Pamela Saletri Parron

We were invited to Patricia's wedding and were informed of proper gifts and the etiquette of the event. We met more missionaries from other places, their kids, and some Spaniards who attended churches of the same denomination but had met in other places in the *comunidad* (province) of Madrid. We met new friends and ate new foods. The wedding dinner lasted about three hours. We did not sit with Antonio and Ricardo, and I'm glad we didn't; those friendships and their insights became invaluable. From those friendships, I came to know the missionaries from a suburb on the other side of Madrid. Through those friendships, I had the opportunity to see where Antonio spent his Sundays. Those missionaries had had an enormous impact on his life, and he felt a desire to help them start this new church plant in the suburban city of Móstoles.

About a week after the wedding, one of our new friends invited us on a day trip to a historical location with the young people from the Móstoles church. She was a Spanish national who attended the American Christian school and ended up not going on the trip because she had to take her PSAT that day. So there we were with the guys again, and I suspected this was causing problems. My suspicions were confirmed that day as I talked to one of the missionaries. She became my great friend and confidant. I found out that there were good reasons behind my suspicions. American students had visited before leaving a trail of broken hearts in their wake. I adamantly denied these charges and examined my memories. Had we initiated anything? Yes, we had accepted invitations, but were we leading them on to believe anything but friendship? The answer stared me in the face as yes since we had accepted these exclusive dates so to speak. However, my conscience was clear in another area; they were seeking us out, not vice versa. In fact, I had made sure to interact with everyone especially the children and young people.

Another thought frightened me. Up until that point, I hadn't been sure if he wanted more than friendship, but this heart-to-heart conversation seemed to confirm that he did. I had noticed Antonio was looking at me more and more in the rearview mirror.

I always looked away not because I wasn't interested but because I was terrified.

Proverbs 4:23 (NIV) says, "Above all else, guard your heart, for everything you do flows from it." Song of Solomon 3:5 (NIV) says, "Do not arouse or awaken love until it so desires." Was the timing right? These verses swirled in my head. I was eighteen and about to make a decision that could have changed my life. I had to stop seeing Antonio socially and determine to return home and let my time in Spain be a pleasant memory or continue moving in a direction that could one day end up with me at Antonio's side, which would mean becoming not a missionary but a Spaniard in my daily life ... for the rest of my life.

I thought about my parents and brother. I knew that God had given me such a myriad of experiences of places and people plus an ability to blend into others' expectations that I was confident I could adjust to Spain as easily as anywhere I had in the States. But what was the *right* decision? "Children, obey your parents in the Lord, for this is right" (Ephesians 6:1 NIV). My parents had given clear instructions about dating. "Lord, I know that people's lives are not their own; it is not for them to direct their steps" (Jeremiah 10:23 NIV). I thought that my parents would be so impressed with Antonio if they knew him. What if this was God's will for my life after all and I threw it away just because of a nationality? Weren't we all citizens of heaven, which superseded all other earthly loyalties? "Search me, God, and know my heart; test me and know my anxious thoughts. See if there is any offensive way in me, and lead me in the way everlasting" (Psalm 139:23–24 NIV). I could twist information and therefore justify my decisions in either direction. I needed God to intervene and answer clearly. I prayed, fasted, and took long walks during the week. I even skipped a few classes.

I had a long list of reasons to continue my relationship with Antonio; I thought it could be the one for me. But I was still very hung up about my size. We were the same height, but I was bigger. I looked around at all the beautiful, petite Spanish women and wondered why in the world he had chosen me. He did not seem to notice that I literally towered above other women. When he looked at me, I felt I was the most beautiful person in the world. So what was I to do? Should I fixate on a point I knew to be superficial and ignore all the personal and spiritual qualities I was so drawn to?

And he was a Spaniard. My parents had spoken of cultural differences that would present problems in the future though I was sure I would be flexible because I was the one who would take on that change. Even so, could God bless a relationship that was a direct violation of my parents' admonition? The last journal entry I wrote before I received an answer read, "I don't want to mess things up. I want to always remain in God's will … 'All things work together for good for they that love the LORD' (Romans 8:28 NIV)."

Sitting next to Antonio at the church in Móstoles the following Sunday, I was lost in prayer. It was one of those prayers that seem to happen when people have no more words left, the groaning of their souls that the Holy Spirit intercedes to God for. Out of nowhere, God reminded me of that lone duck that quacked in the night. The words *a Spanish teacher* echoed in my recollection with new meaning. I tried not to cry. And then peace, that amazing peace of a burden lifted, a restricted heart allowed to breathe freely, a soul that could feel joy again flooded me. Silent tears slid through my fingers. Not being an overly sentimental person on the outside, I tried my best to control my emotion and tucked my God moment away so I could savor it later.

I said nothing to Antonio. I simply took my guard down. So did he. We discussed the future, our plans and dreams. We drew closer. He asked Ricardo to sit in the back seat with Sara so we could be up front. We always said hello and goodbye to everyone in the church in the same way— two kisses, one on each cheek that was more of a cheek to cheek with smooching sounds than actual kisses. But goodbyes between Antonio and me started taking longer, and he placed his kisses right on my cheeks. With every goodbye, they got closer to my mouth.

One evening in November, after a long day of activity and talking, he entwined his fingers in mine, and we walked hand in hand as we continued to talk in the park. That goodbye at our front door took forever, but we both knew. He kissed me that night as Sara and Ricardo awkwardly observed the stars. Antonio never got down on one knee and asked me to marry him. Thankfully, that had never been a dream of mine. We knew that that kiss that day was the promise of a life together. What had felt like forever had actually happened in five weeks.

I had one huge confession to make to my parents along with a request. I wished to extend my time in Spain. My parents were terribly disappointed with my decision to pursue a relationship with Antonio. I was eighteen; what did I know about life for the long haul? They told me I had to come home when I was scheduled to come home and that I was to concentrate on my studies. I tried to make them see Antonio through my eyes. They insisted that he sounded like a wonderful young man but that this was not the time or the place. I cried for hours and prayed. I related the news to Antonio and his family while fighting back tears. His mother took my hands and gently told me that she understood my parents completely and not to be upset with them. Then she took Antonio's hands with mine between her own and simply said that if it was God's will that we be together, we would be. It was a time to be patient and wait.

We made the most of the month we had left. One of my favorite memories was being in a rowboat on a lake in a park while Antonio played the guitar and sang. We had a picnic in the park, and everything was perfect, right out of a romance novel.

I left Spain on Christmas Eve day, also Antonio's birthday. He kissed my tears and kissed me goodbye with a promise to write and to learn English so he could ask my father for his permission to marry me the next summer.

When I arrived in Chicago, my family was waiting. There was a huge storm, and we also had car trouble. We spent Christmas Eve in a motel, and Christmas Day consisted of the presents I had brought from Spain. We had dinner at Denny's, the only place open on Christmas Day. We had a lot of time to talk. A church member made the six-hour drive down to rescue us and then another six hours to bring us home.

My parents were glad to have me back, and it was good to be home. All too soon I had to return to college. I was determined to squeeze in as many classes as I could to complete my degree in two instead of the traditional three years that remained. I wanted to return to Antonio and Spain as soon as possible.

Sara and I were again roommates, and we plunged back into the academic routine along with a few adventures. Mostly it was hard work. Go to class. Sleep. Go to work. Study. Sleep a couple hours. Repeat. Sara and I decorated our room to remind us of Spain ... and Antonio and Ricardo. True to his word, Antonio wrote me every day. I couldn't give up; I had to keep on going. In the days before Teaching English as a Second Language or English Language Learners degrees were more mainstreamed, I began to volunteer teaching English at a community center to gain experience. I volunteered as an assistant teaching Spanish in after-school enrichment classes for elementary children alongside a high school Spanish teacher. I also began attending a small Spanish-speaking church where I could practice the language of my love and future life.

The people in that church became a family to me. They invited me into their homes and fed me. They were not perfect people; they lived simply, but it was heaven to me. I watched them open their homes and help others including me. There were several so-called mixed couples—Americans married to people from other countries. I listened to their stories and talked about mine while observing how beautifully God worked through these people. Many had never been to college or a seminary, but faith, prayer, song, and Bible verses were woven into their cores. It was a wonderful time because my life felt like it had purpose and direction.

My only regret was that my parents seemed disappointed that my relationship with Antonio had not faded but had grown stronger.

Antonio was coming to visit me that summer, and I could not have been more pleased. I prayed that my family would see through the language barrier and see the man I saw. With about a week to go before my summer classes ended, I became quite sick. I was typing my final papers and throwing up and typing in a tortuous cycle. I felt so weak that I crashed at a friend's house while desperately working to finish my final reports. Under my friend's care, I somehow finished everything.

Feeling better and with school complete, I put in as many hours as I could at my job as shift manager at the pizza place. The night before I left to pick up Antonio in Chicago, I turned in my keys to the restaurant to my boss. I assured him I would be back in September. The next morning, I packed up and headed to Chicago. After six months of waiting, there he was!

I was so excited to see Antonio that I forgot where I had parked. He was exhausted from the trip, and there we were wandering all over one of O'Hare's parking complexes trying to find my bright orange Plymouth Horizon. I was embarrassed as could be, but we finally found it and began the six-hour drive home. Antonio fell asleep. I had him sitting next to me! It was almost strange to see him outside Spain, but I was so happy. As was my habit, I prayed and daydreamed as I drove.

My mom was waiting for us; my dad and brother were at church camp from which we would pick them up the next day. Antonio had picked up some English but not enough for him to maintain a conversation comfortably, so I translated most of the time.

After spending time at our place and visiting my grandparents on the golf course and my aunt and uncle on the farm, we were going camping as a family to Copper Harbor, Michigan, next to Lake Superior. Camping was our family thing. We had a dining tent, my parents had a tent, and Eric, Antonio, and I had individual pup tents. It was there that Antonio officially asked my dad for my hand in marriage and our engagement became official. In that beautiful place, we sat on the shore of the lake and prayed and dedicated our lives to God and to each other.

After a week, we broke camp. The plan was to stop by the house to do laundry and resupply before taking a casual road trip to St. Louis to see Sara and her family. It was a bright, sunny day. My ring was glistening on my finger with the movements of packing the tent when I started to shake with fever and feel sick. I shook with chills and fitfully slept most of the way home except when we stopped so I could be sick. I was too weak to climb the stairs to my room by the time we got home. Antonio stayed by my side as I continued to shake and doze on and off. He kept telling me that I needed to go to a hospital. I wasn't processing any information. My mom remembered that my contacts were still in my eyes in the middle of the night and walked me to the bathroom to take them out. When we turned on the lights, we noticed that my arms had bruising in a spiderweb pattern all over. Perhaps this wasn't the flu after all.

CHAPTER 4

Painful Reckoning

Afour-hundred-pound weight must have been set on head; the pressure was unbearably intense. My eyelids wouldn't stay open. I was trying to wake up but couldn't. Light and forms without clarity were what I perceived, but that awful heaviness in my head drew me back to unconsciousness, into this unnatural suffocating feeling of being trapped by impenetrable darkness. I regained consciousness from this state bit by bit, one thought at a time. Awareness came in random thoughts that I could not process. I suddenly was struck by the sensation of my front teeth being pushed out at a 90 degree angle and thinking what that must look like and what my dentist would say.

In another thought, I became aware of pizza, that everyone was going to eat pizza. I never saw, smelled, or touched it, but it was a part of my strange awakening consciousness. Then slowly, the pain in my throat took precedence over all the other painful sensations, and I had a desperate need for water. The sensation of the dryness and pain overwhelmed me; I had no other thoughts. I couldn't speak. It was like being in a bad dream from which I just could not make myself wake up. I am sure I tried to move to get someone's attention that I needed help. I remember voices and that people were around me, but I have no clear memory, just blurred and unfocused images mixed with confusion.

Slowly, yellow figures take shape as people and beeps and clicks around me make me realize that I'm in a hospital, but not the hospital in Neillsville. I finally understand the pain in my throat and the initial sensations regarding my teeth are the result of a breathing tube, and I'm told I have to breath on my own before I can drink or talk. I'm told to relax and breathe. I'm told the machine will breathe for me only when I can't. Inhale. Exhale.

I'm so tired.

Inhale.

Why is this so hard?

Ultimately, the machine kicks in to give me air, and the process resumes. Then strange, unnatural sleep follows.

Every time I woke up a little, I thought that I was in a different room and that the people were all covered up. I had no concept of time though days had passed. After what felt like an eternity, that horrible tube was pulled from my throat causing searing pain. Warm, moist, artificial, rubbery-smelling air followed when a mask was put over my nose and mouth. Up until then, I had been lying mostly flat on my back. The head of the bed was elevated slightly, and I was propped up a little. I could see, but I could not understand. I had tubes everywhere. I hurt all over. I could hardly move.

Eventually, I grasped that I was in a hospital in Madison, Wisconsin, and that I had been there for a while. I asked what the date was and didn't question the missing time but instead worried and hoped I would be out of the hospital five days from then on my nineteenth birthday and be able to do things with Antonio.

I don't remember questioning the fact that I hadn't been to the bathroom for a long time, but I let the nurse know that I was close to that time of the month and didn't want to make a mess. She came close, and I could tell she was smiling beneath her mask. She lightly touched my shoulder with her gloved hand as she bent down as if to tell me a secret. "You really don't need to worry about that."

I had no memory of what had happened since that early morning drive to the Neillsville hospital. Ten days earlier, on August 13, 1988, I had been flown by helicopter from our small country hospital to Madison University Hospital, where I could be put on life support. I was quickly put in an isolation room in the intensive care unit. My body had all but shut down. Shortly after my arrival, I had stopped responding in any manner. A grand mal seizure signaled that death was close to winning one more time over life. The medical teams continued to fight for my young life. Tubes were inserted, machines were hooked up, and drugs were administered.

Antonio and my parents had watched the helicopter fly away before they drove home, about a twenty-minute trip. They told my brother what was happening, and then everyone packed bags and headed to Madison, about a three-hour drive. My body was so full of fluids that by the time my family arrived several hours later, the body on the bed was nearly unrecognizable. My unseeing eyes were covered with a protective gel because I was too bloated to be able to close them. The doctors informed my family that I had only about a 10 percent chance of living through this trauma. They also cautioned them that if I lived, my body had suffered significant damage from which I would not recover. They refused to entertain speculations about what that entailed and simply continued focusing on my survival. My mom, dad, and brother lived in the emergency room waiting room with Antonio, who was getting a crash course in English.

Their despair was far worse than mine. They were helpless to even be with me except in protective gear for limited hours and then only two people at a time. I was told that they talked to me, prayed over me, and read psalms and that Antonio sang to me. Before they had left home for Madison, they made many calls for prayers. Prayers were being lifted up on my behalf. Sara and her parents, whose home we were to have visited in St. Louis, immediately drove up to Madison. Friends and family came to help my parents, brother, and Antonio find a place to sleep and to make sure they ate something. (The pizza I had imagined was the opportunity seized to get them to eat in celebration of "We think she's going to make it!'") God graciously provided people who spoke Spanish for Antonio to be able to understand what could be understood during those critical first two weeks.

Meanwhile, I became increasingly aware of the pain in the rest of my body and more important that I didn't have any clothes on, no hospital gown, nothing, nada. There were too many tubes and wires to make even a gown practical to wear. Groups of doctors and their medical students dressed in protective gear crammed in and then left the little room talking as though I weren't there about things I wasn't able to understand. Whenever I was covered by a blanket, the doctors unceremoniously uncovered me to discuss my condition. I was unable to cover myself back up, but thankfully, the nurses and my family were good about doing that for me. I somehow managed to move my hand to my chest in one of those moments of consciousness.

"My hands ... What had happened to my hands?"

Some of my fingers were black and stiff. *Like a mummy,* I thought. I saw patches of dark red, purple, and black all over my arms. Then I came to understand that the doctors with their groups would come in and uncover my legs because they had suffered the same damage as my hands had. They probed my legs; I wasn't aware of their touch in some places, I felt the slight pressure of their touch in other places, and I felt hideous pain when they touched other spots. The drugs I was on and the shock of the physical trauma affected my judgment; what still worried me the most was not my physical condition but my nakedness and inability to cover myself.

When I was alone, which was a rarity, I examined my hands as best as I could. I examined the stiff, black, dead fingers that included my nails. My eyes followed to the places where the blackness turned into a deep purple and then to places where it was an angry, hot red and then to places with normal coloring as it connected to living tissue. *Could this be me? Are these my hands?* I slowly began to understand that there was something seriously wrong. I was not recovering from a bad flu or an intense bout of pneumonia.

Meningococcal meningitis/septicemia had almost killed me.

After two weeks, I watched the ceiling tiles and fluorescent lights go by as I was transferred to a curtained section of the burn unit to deal with my dead and damaged tissue. Everyone was masked and had his or her hair covered; they were gowned, gloved, and footied at all times. Everyone had to be protected from the bacteria in my system; I felt I was the disease.

The membranes covering and protecting the brain and spinal cord—the meninges—become infected and swell in those who contract meningococcal meningitis. The symptoms include sudden onset of fever, headache, stiff neck, nausea, vomiting, increased sensitivity to light, and confusion. During this stage of the illness, I thought I had a bad flu. The fever was sudden and high, I was shaking, and my teeth were chattering with cold when we were driving home. (Here's my medical advice and a disclaimer—I am not a trained professional in this matter. If you are an adult and have a high fever, go to the doctor immediately.)

Unbeknown to us then, the meningococcal infection was entering my bloodstream, which in my case became a more serious form of septicemia—meningococcemia. With meningococcal septicemia, the bacteria enter the bloodstream, multiply, damage the blood vessels, and cause bleeding into the skin and organs. At that point, fatigue, vomiting, cold hands and feet, cold chills, severe aches and pain in the muscles, joints, chest or abdomen, rapid breathing, and diarrhea occur.

In the later stages, a dark purple rash develops. Due to the damage to the blood vessels, someone with this condition could die of internal hemorrhaging. According to the CDC,

> Meningococcal septicemia is very serious and can be fatal. In fatal cases, deaths can occur in as little as a few hours. In nonfatal cases, permanent disabilities can include amputation of toes, fingers, or limbs or severe scarring as a result of skin grafts.[3]

Basically, the disease had run its course in about forty-eight hours. That was when I began the long process of recovery—sifting through the damage to find out if anything was recoverable, clear out the damaged parts, and piece back together whatever remained. My case of meningococcemia would be categorized as a nonfatal case. The CDC's website's one-sentence long description would require boxes of chart notes, months of hospitalization, hundreds of liters of blood, pain beyond description, and tears beyond counting. I would not make it home for my birthday.

I had woken up from my coma to a nightmare. Even after my survival seemed sure, doctors remained elusive, cautious, and factual concerning what would happen next. I had a lot of dead and damaged tissue in unknown and varying degrees, and so it would be necessary to treat me much like a burn victim. I was in a bed in a curtained area of the burn unit. I couldn't see other patients, nurses, or doctors, but I heard and smelled them. Visitors were still limited and had to be in protective gear along with everyone else.

The process began of separating what was alive from what was dead before gangrene worked its own poison into my system. It was painfully obvious that some of my fingers had to go. They were actually grossing me out, and I just wanted to get it over with. I would lose my pinky fingers at the nub, and my middle and index fingers on my left hand would be partially amputated at the second knuckle. However, it was far more complicated than that. My skin was a patchwork of blotches ranging from black to pink, from dead to damaged to fine, and sorting that out took time and tests.

Simply put, here was the test. If you poke some skin with something sharp and it hurts and bleeds, it's alive. If it just bleeds, it's damaged. If it hurts and sort of bleeds, it's damaged. If it doesn't hurt or bleed, it's dead. One of many problems was that the surface could look just fine but there could be severe damage below that and vice versa. In places, the damage was just skin deep; in other places, it went much deeper. I was taken to two machines to get images. I asked everyone if they thought I was going to lose my legs because different groups of doctors would come in, examine my legs and feet, and discuss them in technical terms and in hushed whispers. From my perspective, my feet looked bad, but I could move my toes. It was so confusing.

Later on, I would better understand, but at that point, I was having a hard time with the fact that the doctors weren't decisive. I mean, I had watched TV; what about all the innovations of modern medicine? How could the doctors not know or even agree on the course of action? It was quite disconcerting to someone in her first year of adulthood. But I knew that my friends and family were praying for a miracle, a full recovery.

On the upside, my kidneys were starting to do their thing without assistance. On the downside, I was discovering how a bedpan works or doesn't. Another positive was that I could wear a hospital gown. Every morning, the burn nurses scrubbed my wounds, cleaned me up, changed my sheets with me in the bed, and finally gave me fifteen minutes to recover whatever dignity I could before Antonio or others came in. My family and friends read letters, told me about phone calls and what Doctor So and So had told them, and generally tried to encourage me. By afternoon, my fever would be raging, and I would be shaking with cold until the fever broke; then I would be sweating buckets. So the cycle continued.

I asked questions and listened intently to prepare myself for what would happen with my feet. Plastic surgeons would come in, bend down to point at them, and discuss the matter. Vascular surgeons stood stoically with arms crossed. Gloved orthopedic surgeons checked the movement of my feet. I have come to the conclusion that talking to most surgeons is an exercise in frustration for them and patients. Although words were spoken, I cannot say that I took away any definable answer. I pleaded with my nurses to give me their opinions on the topic of whether I would lose my legs, but they simply told me they had no idea. I certainly had no idea, just hopes.

Some machines were brought to me, and I was taken to other machines to determine the actual amount of damage to my legs. I prayed anxious prayers. During one of the tests on my feet, when everyone left the room for the big machine to penetrate my skin with whatever kind of radiation it was this time, I knew.

I just knew.

Tears flowed from my eyes and pooled in my ears as I lay there. The devastating knowing was then overwhelmed by the peace of God's presence. It wasn't an audible voice; it was a peace that enveloped me in God's presence. In that moment, the anxiousness caused by the indecision just evaporated, and God communicated to me that I was going to lose my legs but that it was all right. For the first time since I had woken up in this nightmare, peace and relief washed over me. My dad always read a psalm and prayed with me before they left for the evening. I told him that evening what I had experienced earlier in the day; I told Antonio too.

The pain in their eyes was unbearable. After they left, the nurses began my evening wound care, which was not as intense as the morning sessions but painful all the same. After everyone left, I lay there in the artificial attempt at darkness still illuminated by artificial light and surrounded by my curtains. I filled my ears with the tears I dared not share with anyone.

I tried to keep my thoughts focused on the present. I imagined patterns in the ceiling panels. I stared at a TV screen without thinking. I concentrated on breathing deeply and slowly to change the flashing numbers on my monitor. Anything to distract me from the physical pain and the overload of information I heard and saw. I could not reconcile what was happening to me … with me. Despite observing everything, I was in disbelief or perhaps attempting to disconnect from what was happening to me. Although these events took place in about a week's time, I remember it as being so much longer.

In the end, the vascular surgeon, Dr. H, seemed to take control of events. He first explained to my family and then to me that surgery had been scheduled for the amputations, a day after my nineteenth birthday. Many questions were asked with very unsatisfying answers.

When I put my *X* on the signature lines of the surgery consent forms, I was legally a conscious adult. I understood that the operation would be long and exploratory in nature. The goal was to leave as much of me intact as possible. We knew that the fingers and both feet had to be removed; however, depending on the damage underneath the big black blotches on my wrists, there was the possibility that I might lose one or both hands as well. It was the same story with my legs as they also had blotches of dead and dying skin tissue; I could lose one or both legs above the knee.

Dr. H explained in his matter-of-fact manner that he would not close any wound created in the removal of dead tissue in any more than a rudimentary way so that the daily debridement procedures would have a greater level of success. Debridement is the removal of dead (necrotic) and/or infected tissue or foreign objects in a wound. But success was not guaranteed; a limb might have to be removed in a later surgery if the debridement processes were unsuccessful.

Waiting is the worst. Waiting for something you want is difficult. Waiting for something you dread is dreadful, full of every negative emotion you can imagine or you want to add to the mix. It was bad enough to wait alone, but when you're looking at people you love who are on the brink of tears and trying to comfort you and make sure you're all right, it's overwhelmingly dreadful. I looked at my hands trying to wrap my head around what they would look like when the fingers were gone.

I wanted to trust in God. I wanted to be a good witness for Jesus by the way I responded to what was happening. I did my best to be pleasant and patient; I knew everyone was trying to help me. I had tried to make everyone comfortable and assure them I was all right. I had prayed a lot especially through the long hours of the early morning. Sleep was welcome, but it was unnatural and interrupted by bad dreams. I heard others' real nightmares through the curtains and the beeping and monitoring of my and everyone else's machines. I prayed a lot. I even allowed thoughts about how it wouldn't be so bad. I had watched TV and had seen people using artificial arms and legs.

I prayed I wouldn't cry as my dad prayed and as Antonio tenderly kissed me and fought back tears. Everyone hovered around my bed with faith, love, and affection before they took me past those doors to the operating theater. I prayed as I bit the inside of my cheek that when they transferred me to the cold, hard operating table, I would have the strength to face this moment and not cry. I prayed as I smelled the stale, rubber-scented air until I started the countdown. "Ten ... nine ... eight ..."

I screamed at the top of my lungs. I heard impatient and upset voices as I was transferred to the right bed. The gentle, yellow-gloved hands of my nurse stroked my cheek and hair as she spoke soothingly to me when she saw I was conscious. Several gowned figures lifted my body again to position me correctly and elevate the stumps where my legs abruptly ceased to be. My screams were capable of waking up everyone in the hospital, but my throat was again burning even with the moist air of the oxygen mask. I think all they heard was me moaning loudly. I felt like they had cut off my legs with a guillotine. I felt overwhelming pain, but there were many other sensations demanding my brain to recognize their urgent messages. My nurse was saying my name and assuring me the morphine was on its way. Consciousness gave way to strange dreams.

I woke again to Antonio's soothing voice close to my head. I hurt so badly. If I tried to move, it was even worse. They tried to get me to eat. I couldn't. I looked at my hands and where my feet used to be expecting to see blood, but there were just wads of bandages around my hands and two big lumps that were propped up on pillows halfway down the bed under the covers. I was having a very hard time processing any information. I just knew I hurt everywhere. I lived breath to breath; it was all I could manage with every ounce of physical and emotional strength I had.

The next morning, two nurses came in with trays of instruments, bandages, and ointments. They had gauze pads galore and bottled, sterile, saline water. Their job was to unwrap the old bandages, clean the open wounds, apply the medicated ointment, and apply new gauze. It all started with morphine going into my IV. The same principles applied as before: bleeding and pain signified living tissue while no bleeding and unfeeling tissue meant dead tissue, which is toxic and must be removed. The problem was that live tissue and dead tissue were side by side.

I stared at my nubs where the dead fingers had been attached just hours before. True to his word, Dr. H had left the nubs open to cover them with skin grafts later. He made the nubs as long as possible to help me grip things better in the future. I was thankful to have any part of my hands left, and I understood the motivation behind what they had done, but I was having trouble just getting through the moment. Waves of nausea rolled over me from the shock, from the blood, from the morphine, from the pain. I fixed my eyes on some point and concentrated on it. When one hand was done, a little more morphine was put in and then work began on the other hand. I stared at the strands of tendons in my wrist. Then the left leg.

This can't be me.

My leg looked like something in a horror movie. I was shaking uncontrollably and begging them to stop. More morphine. Finally, the right leg, and after seeing the left leg, I thought this one didn't look as bad; it was covered with more skin. When they lifted my leg and I could breathe again, I asked about my knee. I was informed that the part I was asking about was my patella tendon. They explained that we had to be very careful not to let it dry out and that Dr. H was concerned about it but was hoping for the best. I focused on my spot on the ceiling again and clenched my teeth. I think I heard and comprehended up until I heard "tendon." I started shaking again as they informed me they were almost finished. Then they rolled me on my right side. And they went to work on my left hip and backside. I caught a glimpse of my hip. At that point, I had to focus out the window or up the wall. I felt my tears drip over the bridge of my nose. I was cleaned up, the bed sheets changed, the floor and bed cleaned up, and I was left alone for about fifteen minutes so I could cry. Then I needed another ten minutes to collect my dignity. My nurse always asked if I was ready before she let anyone come visit. I knew it would take another five minutes for a visitor to put on the protective gear. Without realizing it, I began putting on mine as well.

Debridement treatments occurred in the morning before visitation and in the evening after visitation ended. In the middle of the day during visitation, I tried to be brave and engage positively with those around me. I also tried to sleep. In the middle of the night, I tried not to think too much and sleep. Rarely was I successful on either account for very long.

Antonio had stayed well past his original departure date. He wanted to stay, but I wanted him to go. He kept talking about finding a job there and taking care of me. I tried to discourage him by saying that there was nothing for him to do for me at that time. He needed to go home so he wouldn't lose his job as an industrial delivery driver, and besides, his family was worried about him. Eric had gone home; school had started for him. Almost a month had gone by since I had entered the hospital. It was hard to comprehend that the world just kept moving forward.

Every moment was agony. After being in the burn unit, I no longer questioned why there was fire in hell. During cleaning treatments, I heard others screaming obscenities at the nurses and others moaning loudly. Some tried to be brave. The majority were unconscious. How I envied them. Most of the voices were present for only a few days. The burn unit was used as an overflow when the ICU was filled. More than once in the wee hours, an overdose victim would be brought in. I heard things that made me forget my pain and pray for others besides me and mine. I probably heard a lot more than I should have.

I believed God heard my prayers; that was a source of hope in the middle of this valley of the shadow of death. Death happened next to me more than once ... a flurry of activity and beeping and urgency only to be replaced by silence, a void in the sounds that should have been. After a while, there were the sounds of a bed unlocking and the curtains swaying, evidence of the bed and the body being removed. Emptiness remained. Tears would fill my ears. I talked to God a lot. The minutes of each day ticked by in slow motion; the nights went by even slower mocking me in prolonging the dread of another cleaning in the morning.

Then one day, an empty bed was rolled into the curtained area next to mine. I heard the compassionate voices of nurses and the resident doctors, even the most jaded among them. They were talking to a four-year-old I'll just call Anna who while making macaroni and cheese by herself had spilled the boiling water down her armpit and side. She would be another patient in the burn unit in need of debridement treatments and skin grafting.

No family member accompanied her. She was alone. She did not speak. She was alone with masked strangers who were trying to comfort her. She cried quietly. The nurses felt that my mother hovered too much over me. They also noticed that she would adopt and encourage families in the waiting room. Between what I heard and my mother's updates from the waiting room, I was often able to piece together stories about what was happening around me. Well, here was a little girl in dire need of a hovering mother. The little curtained space with one bed became a bigger curtained space with two beds. The nurses brought movies for Anna and I to watch. Antonio fed me, and my mom fed Anna. Sometimes, I would see her just staring at me. I would smile at her and say something. She started smiling back. We were the only ones whose whole faces we could see since everyone else had only eyes showing over their masks. We were both threatened with feeding tubes because we weren't eating enough. Oh the irony!

One slow day, they masked and covered us and took us and all our tubes and bags and bottles with me still in my bed out to the helicopter pad so we could enjoy the warm fall day for fifteen minutes. Anna and I smiled at the big fuss, production, and fanfare of our two-patient parade. It was the first time I had seen some people's faces.

Another distraction was the day the nurses included Anna and me on a prank they played on Dr. H. He wore black horn-rimmed reading glasses when reviewing charts, so the nurses drew replica shapes of Dr. H's glasses on plastic lab goggles with a black marker. As soon as they knew he was coming, they came in and strapped the goggles on us and themselves. Anna actually giggled, and I think I did too. The ever-stoic Dr. H looked at all of us as if we were all preposterous and took a deep breath. He did not giggle, but he almost smiled, and there was definitely more lightness in his face and a twinkle in his eyes.

I had to be brave. I would not cry out. And I was listening. The curtain was closed for morning treatments. Anna had started to speak. "Pam, are dey scrubbin'?" *Scrubbing* was how I had referred to it once when we were talking about debridement, and the term stuck. I swallowed to make my voice steady and answered her. I heard the fear in her voice as her nurses were getting her trays ready and talking to her in soothing tones. She cried less than the construction worker on the other side of the unit.

Anna and I ended up with feeding tubes stuffed down our noses. That was gruesome. But when the curtain opened, I batted at the pink tube with my bandaged right mitt and asked her if she had gotten a pink elephant trunk too. Her dark lashes were wet with tears, but she liked that and smiled, and that's what we called them from then on.

The day before our surgeries, we were lifted into the stainless-steel tub. She went first and then sat with the nurses at their station while I was in the tub. The warm water was a balm, but the rest was horrific. Being moved was always traumatic; it didn't matter if it was to use the bedpan, change position, or whatever. To be put in the tub was to be placed on a cold, flat slab that replaced the forks of a forklift on this transfer apparatus with wheels. It was on this slab that my awkwardly placed (and thankfully mostly covered) body was rolled past the nurses' station to the tub and then none too smoothly lowered into the medicine-laced water. I touched some of the wounds and watched how my blood swirled and mixed with the water. They came to get me out, but I asked for more time. I loved the water, but this surreal image would remain in my dreams to this day. I don't remember tears, just drifting into nothingness.

"Pruney Pam!" A nurse playfully teased in the background. A giggle followed, and the echo of "Pwuney Pam!" of a four-year-old rang out and brought me back to the present with the shaking of my head and a smile.

The curtains were closed between us as we lay there in the artificial darkness, but I heard her quiet sobs. "Anna honey, what's wrong?" I asked. I realized it was a ridiculous question, but I couldn't stay silent. She was four.

Her answer broke my heart. "I want my mommy. Where's my mommy?" I knew that one of the nurses was trying to adopt her as her family was under serious investigation. I asked a nurse to open the curtain between us so we could at least see each other. As I watched Anna fall asleep still sniffling, I was reminded that there were so many situations that were much worse than mine.

My IV site was burning and becoming swollen. The previous night, I had told the nurse that whatever was in that little bag was burning my vein. I was ignored. It was the morning of the operation and I was listening to Dr. H, another new resident, and my regular nurses discussing the fact that I needed a new IV site. You might think that at that point, the prospect of a simple IV would leave me unfazed, but that was not the case. The antibiotic that was to drip slowly into my system over two hours had entered my system in twenty minutes and had burned through one of the few precious veins I had left. After having nurses and residents attempting to start an IV simultaneously on both arms for I don't know how long, Dr. H insisted that I be transported to surgery to let the anesthesiologist offer solutions.

The anesthesiologist and resident told me that they were going to start an IV in my neck. I could not hold back the floodgates. I was sobbing, begging them to use a butterfly needle to just put me to sleep (a ridiculous suggestion) and then put the IV in wherever they wanted. The residents and nurses were just a few years older than me, and I think they felt sorry for me as the anesthesiologist assured me that he put this type of IV in every day. I managed to choke out, "But I don't!"

By some miracle, he went over my arms again and found a vein that worked. Meanwhile, my resident promised me this would never happen again and that they were going to surgically put in a Hickman catheter in a vein near my heart. They would not have to start another IV or draw blood every morning from my arms anymore; they could get it from the port. That was my happy thought as I counted back, "Ten, nine, eight …"

Oh how I hated waking up. Unconsciousness was sweet relief. Even being slightly conscious was to be tormented by so many pain messages. I thought I was going to lose my mind and any ability to control my reactions. Different people have different reactions to pain relievers. Why they are called that is beyond me as they do not relieve pain.

My experience told me that morphine is a pain confounder. While the patient is aware of the pain, the mind is unable to process it and react. Morphine relieves pain only when enough of it is administered so that you can drift off into a stupefied sleep. No more sleep for me. I was being forced back to consciousness after another ten-hour procedure. I was back in my bed in my curtained area. A burning sensation in my left inner thigh was pushing to the front of my befuddled mind. I caught sight of a lamp under my sheet. My nurse was trying to get me to stop thrashing my arms around … something about skin grafts.

I slowly begin to make sense of my situation. My hands and wrists had been covered with grafted skin from my thigh. The top layer of the donor site had been shaved off, an area about two and a half inches by eight inches. The skin does not scab over when the top layer of the dermis is removed, so a special piece of fabric covered the site. With the help of my oozing plasma and the heat lamp, an artificial scab would form that would peel off when the skin underneath had healed. The good news is that the pain from this site would subside in a few days to a bearable level, but at that moment, it was a hot mess.

The donor skin from my leg had to be cut to size and stitched onto the open wounds on my nubs, fingers, and wrists. My heart sank when I caught a glimpse. I don't know exactly what I was expecting, but it wasn't what I saw. I had watched TV. Didn't people in the movies have horrific accidents and then have reconstructive surgery that made them even better looking? The nurses took off the bandages, but instead of the beautiful reveal of the movies, well ... The movie that came to mind was *Frankenstein*. More tiny black stitches then I could count holding on patches of almost dead skin to cover the previously opened places. My nurses read my expression like a book and began explaining that it would get better and why.

One of them painstakingly rolled what looked like a large Q-tip over the top of the graft. I really couldn't feel anything except horror until she pushed closer to the stitches. Then there was pain. Basically, my graft was blood- and therefore oxygen-deprived; hence the awful coloring. That would change as the graft adhered to the blood vessels below. No, the skin color and texture would never be the same, but they assured me that the yellowish-green color would be replaced by a purple color and then fade as the years went by. *Years?*

Instead of the debridement cleanings, it would be important to push out any pockets of standing blood. It was crawl-out-of-your-skin uncomfortable but not painful. The procedure took just as much time if not longer than debriding did.

As I stared at my right hand, I saw the port wine stain birthmark on my thumb. When people noticed it, I was always asked, "What happened there?" I had been teased mercilessly through early elementary school that I was a baby who sucked her thumb. I had learned to hold my hands in a way that hid my birthmark from view at least for a while. The irony hit hard. How would I even attempt to hide that big ugly patch on the back of my wrists and the remaining fingers? How could I possibly hide the fact of my missing fingers and the ugly nubs that were left? I already knew how people had reacted to my birthmark and wondered how they would react to this. I had hated shaking hands because that was how most people first noticed my birthmark. How could I ever shake anyone's hand like this?

The nurse started the treatment on my left hand. There was a big patch on my wrist. Then she started on the patches covering my nubs. Not for the first time, I stared at my hand where my fingers should have been. The remaining parts of my hand reminded me of Bif, my brother's pet white rat. Bif contentedly sat on my brother's shoulders when he was working on the computer or watching TV. She was smart and social, and we all ended up liking her a lot once we got used to the tail, the beady red eyes, and those paws with the little claws. My left hand resembled Bif's front left paw sans the claws ... I had my own rat paw as I started referring to it. My left hand had worn an engagement ring just a month earlier. My ring finger and thumb were the only digits that remained on my left hand. Only minutes before, I had been worried about shaking hands, but then I soberly thought about holding Antonio's hand and wearing a beautiful ring on that disfigured hand. It was too difficult to process that this would be me ... for the rest of my life. If I had struggled with body image before, it was nothing compared to the repulsion I was feeling at that time.

The morning of the day after surgery, Dr. H came in and in what would be his way of greeting me from that moment forward, he took my hands, looked them over thoroughly, and nodded his approval. It was obvious he thought they looked good from a surgical point of view at least. For the first time since the day before surgery, the bandages on my legs came off. Horrified shock. My mind and emotions were temporarily paralyzed and numb as my eyes and brain processed the visual overload. The words I heard myself say in a flat tone were somehow disconnected from me.

"What's that moving?"

"That's your muscle."

"What's that yellow in there?"

"That's your fat layer."

"Oh ..."

The pain was horrific as always. The shock of what I saw overwhelmed me. The surgery was to put skin grafts on my hands and the required donor site and to perform more radical surgical debridement. There is a reason it is called radical. Some wounds had almost doubled in size. My legs and left hip were missing large chunks of what used to be me.

About halfway through the treatment, my new resident came in to check on my Hickman port. With everything else, I had forgotten that the nurse hadn't needed to do a blood draw in my arm that morning and had instead taken it from this white tube in my chest. From there, the blood looked black because it was completely oxygen depleted and about to enter the heart, where it would again be infused with oxygen and regain that bright-red color I was used to seeing. With a pink tube in my nose and the white tube in my chest, what more could a girl ask for? He was pleased with himself as my white tube was another success. Unfortunately, I was not feeling successful.

Being young and kind, he asked me how I was doing; Dr. H always asked very precise questions that dealt with the physical reality at hand. Being young and medically inexperienced, I looked at my left leg—what was left of it—and especially at the deep and wide crater above the knee. I didn't want to cry, but I was not being successful. Thank heavens Anna was still heavily sedated. I heard myself force out the bitter question, "Why didn't you just cut the rest of my leg off and get it over with?" There was a pause followed by a deep breath. His tone of voice and gentle answer shamed me because I knew that he hurt for me and that they were not being malicious; they were doing everything they could to minimize my loss and maximize my future success.

It took me a lot longer to collect my dignity before my visitors came in that morning. To top it off, my nurses had to help me blow my nose quite a few times, which is especially disgusting when you have a pink feeding tube in it. I was exhausted physically, emotionally, mentally, and spiritually. I had been in the burn unit for nearly a month. Not a moment had passed when I wasn't in pain—not discomfort but excruciating and unbearable pain, pain that made questions such as "What do you want to drink?" or "Which movie should I put on?" irrelevant. No one asked me how I was doing even as a polite nicety because the truth was too apparent.

Antonio had been with me every day through it all. He assured me and promised me we would get through this. His one month of vacation had stretched to two. He had faithfully sat near my head and caressed my head and shoulder, the only places I could be touched. He had seen my dead fingers and the blotches on my legs and arms, but after my first surgery, I was bundled in clean white bandages. Antonio and my family had no idea what I looked like when the bandages came off. Dr. H and the residents gave them updates, but they did not see the divots and ever-widening, deepening holes in my flesh. They had no idea what I had gone through. I'm sure the process was explained, but they did not see the blood, the muscles, the tendons, and the bone. They did not hear the snipping. They did not smell the decay, the blood, the burning from the cauterizing to stop bleeding. They did not see my horror and pain; the devastation of my body and soul was somewhat hidden from them. Only my nurses knew. I was closing down to everyone but them.

The longer the process continued, the less I could handle trying to maintain relationships with my parents, who I knew loved me, and even to my faithful, loving Antonio. I assured him that there was nothing he could do there. He needed to go home until I recovered. I told him it was pointless to talk about the future until we knew what I would be able to do. So after almost two months in the States, Antonio was driven by my dad to Chicago to fly home in mid-September.

CHAPTER 5

Broken

M y dreams were strange as my mind attempted to override the drugs and process what had happened. A recurring dream was that I was trying to get ready to go to one of my brother's basketball games but was missing part of my feet, so I kept wrapping them tighter and tighter with rolled gauze. The gauze bandages kept coming loose and trailing behind me out of my tennis shoes as I walked in the gym. I started missing more and more of my feet as the dream repeated. I never had any trouble keeping tennis shoes on or walking.

Dreams are weird. I would wake up sweating; I never knew why because my reality made more anatomical sense, but it certainly wasn't any better. As a matter of fact, it was worse; I was still living a nightmare.

Ever since the last surgery, whatever my hopes had been sunk into my present reality. I listened respectfully when my mom and dad read letters and then from the Bible and then prayed before they had to leave before my night cleaning. I had to bear the long night and then my morning cleaning. I was a soul in crisis. I had stopped listening. I had stopped praying. I was not on speaking terms with God. That's not altogether true; I was still making comments to God. However, I didn't want to hear anything except an explanation, maybe an apology. I could have definitely gone for a Bible miracle or intervention. I was barely able to remember that moment when I experienced the peace of God's presence. I thought maybe I had imagined it, and those fiery darts of doubt tormented me. I believed in a sovereign God. I knew what the word sovereign meant.

I was having a difficult time with God at the moment. Why hadn't He let me die? Maybe what some people had implied should be carefully considered. Had I done something to offend Him? Was He angry with me? Why did He remain silent? He could do anything, so why didn't He intervene? I was left to wonder. I related to the psalmist who wrote, "Whom have I in heaven but You?" (Psalm 73:25 NIV). I could not stop believing even if I was discouraged and frustrated. Verse 26 seemed to fit as well: "My flesh and my heart may fail, But God is the strength of my heart."

Up to that point, I had kept the faith in my heart. Some suggested that I needed to make peace with God. Some had asked outright, "What sin has Pam committed for God to punish her in this manner?" I knew that I had sinned more than enough against God and that He had every right to punish me if He desired. During my long nights, I could not avoid thinking about God even though I wanted to. I couldn't stop believing that there was a God, but maybe I had been a disappointment to Him. I knew Jesus died to save me, but maybe I just wasn't living up to His expectations. I whispered in the artificial darkness, "God, forgive me. I'll try harder to do right, no more swearing. God, I'm begging you. Make the pain stop, please God, just for thirty seconds. Just so I can breathe in and out pain free one time. Please God, make it stop."

It did not stop. I wondered again why God didn't just let me die.

My mom read the cards of encouragement people sent. Some were more encouraging than others. I knew that every person who wrote those cards had remembered me and had taken the time to write something and buy a stamp and mail it to me, so I conceded that their hearts were in the right place. Their words, however, were sometimes misplaced, and that was in addition to my heart and mind being shaken up and misplaced in attitude. I've had more time to think about this, and I have to say that there are some situations that are very difficult to say anything about, but we must try to encourage, love, and build others up.

There are several things that happened that really should have been left for a different occasion or at the very least were worth a moment's honest reflection on how a nineteen-year-old in my circumstances might receive such admonitions. Some people instructed me to remember and read the book of Job, but I couldn't feed myself or go to the bathroom by myself. I couldn't even hold a fork or spoon much less a book. I was in terrible pain. *You want me to read Job?* I thought. *You go read Job! I'm living Job!* I'm ashamed to admit it, but I came to hate Romans 8:28 (NIV): "And we know that in all things God works for the good of those who love him, who have been called according to his purpose." I just couldn't see or hear that purpose for my life. I was unable to process any of it for the pain in my body, mind, and soul. I believed in those verses, but I felt that they were being smacked on my forehead as if they would resolve every question and hurt. I felt that my pain was completely overlooked and minimized. It was like putting a Band-Aid on a gaping wound, and I resented it. Those words oversimplified those verses.

Then a letter came from a woman from my childhood, not someone I knew well, but someone whom I remembered as having been very kind to me. We had visited her home several times, and I knew she had been through some very difficult times recently. She included her prayers and Bible verses in her correspondence. It said basically the same thing as Romans 8:28, but her words felt gentle and compassionate. She penned the words from Jeremiah 29:11 (NIV): "For I know the plans I have for you, declares the LORD, plans for welfare and not for evil, to give you a future and a hope." I pictured her speaking to me.

Being the preacher's kid who was at church every time the door opened, I had been present more than once when my dad had done a verse-by-verse study through the Old Testament book of Jeremiah.

While I was not an expert, I was aware of the context of this verse mostly because this chapter was what the prophet Daniel was reading; Daniel has always been one of my favorite Bible persons. I knew the history. Jeremiah was known as the weeping prophet because he had witnessed his prophecy come true.

When he was old, Jerusalem and the magnificent temple Solomon had built were destroyed. Jeremiah was taken against his will to Egypt. His life had begun with such promise. He had been born into the priesthood and began ministering when he was a young man under the last good king, Josiah. He must have hoped and prayed that his people would turn back to God. Over forty years, he watched those hopes dissolve as things went from good to bad to worse and then to total destruction. He faithfully spoke God's truth to the people, but they mistreated him. Other people who spoke from their own intellects and voiced their own opinions were rewarded with positions of influence and affluence while Jeremiah was repeatedly thrown into a pit.

He struggled, but he faithfully held to his calling. The name Jeremiah means one raised up by the Lord, but his message from God was ignored. With his heart breaking, he watched the best and brightest of his people being taken away to a conquering Babylon. I imagine he watched and prayed until they were out of his sight and then he wept and prayed.

Daniel, a teenager, was among those taken away. We know that Daniel received and read the letter Jeremiah wrote in chapter 29 to those in Babylon, a word of assurance from God: "'For I know the plans I have for you,' declares the Lord, 'plans to prosper you and not to harm you, plans to give you hope and a future'" (Jeremiah 29:11 NIV). That was one verse in the middle of a chapter in the middle of a book of pain written thousands of years ago, but those words came over me as though they had been written just for me that God whispered to my heart at just that moment. Once again, I had that peace of His presence with me.

As I lay in my hospital bed that night, those words swirled in my head. My body was still disfigured, I was still in pain, there was still a white tube protruding from my chest and a pink one coming out of my nose, but God had assured me in the peace of His presence that I was not alone or forgotten and that I was loved despite everything. A camp song came to my mind from out of the recesses of memory.

King Jesus is all, my all in all;
And I know that he answers
Me when I call.
Walking by His side,
I'm satisfied.
Cuz King Jesus is all, my all in all.

I had asked for my mom to save that card. Later on, God would speak to me clearly through the next two verses that had been neatly written there.

"For I know the plans I have for you," declares the LORD, "plans to prosper you and not to harm you, plans to give you hope and a future. Then you will call on me and come and pray to me, and I will listen to you. *You will seek me and find me, when you seek me with all your heart.*" (Jeremiah 29:11–13 NIV; emphasis mine)

"Ten, nine, eight, seven ..." I woke up feeling rather nauseous, disoriented, and drugged, but the searing pain was not there. I was still in pain, but this pain was much less than what I had anticipated. I had gone into surgery to be grafted. My first clue should have been that there were no heat lamps, but I was still quite groggy. Finally, after I was able to speak and had stopped slurring my words, I told the nurses that I wasn't feeling as bad as I had expected to. I think I might have even smiled behind the oxygen mask that doubled as a humidifier of sorts to relieve the rawness of my abused trachea.

Breathing tubes were not kind to me. The nurses were rather serious and watching me closely as they carefully explained that I had received temporary skin grafts. This was confusing because I had been made to understand that skin was an organ and that a graft, a transplant of sorts, had to come from the individual himself or herself.

Apparently, Dr. H had decided not to risk losing precious donor sites from my body because he wasn't confident that the tissue underneath was healthy enough to support a graft. So instead, he took the precaution to cover it and let it heal an additional week before the actual skin grafting. Then they stopped talking as if that was the end of the story. I wanted to know what the temporary grafts were. They answered that temporary grafts were either pig skin or cadaver skin that had been medically treated. They continued with their explanation as if that would distract me from what the grafts were made of.

"And mine are …?"

"Cadaver."

"Oh …" It was disturbing. I had a deceased person's skin on me. I was glad I had gone through the horror of what my own grafted skin looked like first because when I saw it on my legs, it didn't look as bad as my own skin had. It was also quite different because instead of being a full-thickness skin graft as those on my hands had been, the grafts on my legs were partial thickness. This had been explained before the operation, so in theory, I knew what to expect.

The donor skin is sent through a machine that makes perforations in it that allow it to then cover an area twice its original size like the paper snowflakes I made as a child. I couldn't stop wondering about the person whose skin I was wearing. I stared out the window and tried to stop thinking. If you've ever tried to stop thinking, you know how successful I was. I ended up watching the numbers and lines on my monitor while just breathing.

I did not have cleanings that week except for my behind, which was a source of great embarrassment to me being exposed like that to everyone—two or three doctors and nurses. The next morning, I was rolled on my right side as per usual. My hands were healing well and were unbandaged, so I put my left hand on my left hip bone for balance. My thumb was pointing to the front and my ring finger was over my wound. I moved my finger to see if I could feel the wound back there and get some idea what it might look like. I relaxed my hand to let my finger drop, but there was no sensation in my finger; I knew I wasn't touching anything. I kept trying to touch bottom if you will, but there was nothing there.

"Bring me a mirror!" I yelled to the approaching footsteps. Yelling in my case was like the barking of a dog that has been debarked; the effort was there but the volume was not. Multiple insertions and removals of breathing tubes had taken their toll. The nurses were reluctant to bring me a mirror, but I was unusually insistent to have it.

After this last surgery, more of me was missing due to more-radical surgical debridement even though I was covered by the temporary grafts. It was visibly apparent to the nurses who had been with me for over a month at that point that this disturbed me although that time I said nothing. They finally found a couple of mirrors and gave me a tour of the crater that now replaced my left bottom. The raw, uneven, gaping flesh filled the mirror. Why I was surprised is beyond me. Ever since I had been moved to the burn unit, my temperature would soar because my body would respond to the toxins and infections caused by yet unseen and unremoved gangrene. Several times when my fever had soared, my visitors would be sent out and a mobile surgical unit would be brought in. I would be rolled on my side and held there while I received morphine. Then they would go to work back there. It wasn't a painful site per se, but I felt the pulling and pushing, heard the comments and snipping, smelled the cauterizing, and recognized the searching eyes that would peer into mine. I would be asked questions by the nurse holding me in place to determine if I had slipped into shock.

I tried to focus and put together the pieces of what I was seeing in the mirror the nurse was holding. Basically, there was a crater back there that my fist could easily disappear into. Hideous and horrifying as it was, I came to understand that this spectacularly gaping space wasn't the source of these bedside procedures. The source of the problem was a hole above the crater itself that was about the size of a quarter that went all the way down to my pelvic bone.

During this show-and-tell session, the resident walked into my curtained space and assessed the scene. After a quick appraisal of the wound area, he assured me that given my temperature stabilizing and the redness and responsiveness of the site, which I called the mine shaft next to the crater, that all dead tissue had been removed. He explained that this site, the quarter-sized shaft, was too deep to be skin grafted but would heal from the bottom up. So we would mark progress by the number of gauze pads that would be stuffed into it; the fewer the number of gauze pads used, the more progress I was making. I heard him, but I wasn't really listening anymore. It was irrelevant at that point. After I had assessed the damage and quietly asked them to back up so that I could see the whole thing at once, I turned back to staring out the window in silence. I was overwhelmed.

The dreams were getting worse. The loose gauze was leaving a bloody trail on the gym floor, and my tennis shoes had fallen off. The people in the bleachers were all staring at me and covering their mouths and whispering. Someone told me that I was making a mess and that I had to leave. I saw my brother's team in their red uniforms huddled around the coach, but my brother was sitting on the bench alone with his head in his hands. I woke up sweating and breathing hard.

Suffering that week came mostly from information and sensory overload. I was beyond being able to feel emotions or think very long about anything before I would just zone out. This was my first taste of this state of being. Before that week, physical pain flooded every part of me. Then, thoughts swept in like vultures. It may seem strange, but there was a huge disconnect between my mind and body, an inability to accept what I saw. I would catch myself thinking, *When this is over* ... Mostly though, I just stayed in the present. Antonio would call and assure me of his love and the plans for our future. I felt more and more distant from him and increasingly felt nothing about anything. I tried to remember that feeling of love but found that remembering the past was almost more painful than thinking about the future. It was beyond painful; it was nearly impossible.

My experiences had happened and were mine, but at that point, I felt disconnected from them; they were distant memories, dreams, or fictional characters. I might as well have died. My heart and mind could not reconcile the person I had been with the reality of the crippled and disfigured person I had become. My past self became irrelevant the moment I woke up from the coma. The future was unimaginable mainly because I was unable to reconcile any imagined scenarios with what the reality of my physical self would be. The future held too many variables and unknowns for me to even consider any possibilities. Dealing with the present often proved to be too much. Even so, I lifted my rat claw to cast a shadow against the white curtain in the background, and I knew how out of place a beautiful ring would be on what was left of that hand.

Thankfully, past beliefs and information did seep through to my consciousness. I still believed there was a God in heaven even at my lowest moments. I believed that Jesus had died on the cross for my sin and that I was saved through Him. I believed that the Holy Spirit was with me. I latched on to the moments in the hospital when I had so clearly felt His presence. I would love to tell you that my faith stood strong, but doubt seeped in. Not about God's existence but concerning His love and goodness and what He expected of me. I talked to God about these things as they came up honestly and in short spurts because of my inability to settle on any one thought for any length of time. I did not read my Bible; I could not hold a book or turn a page. My favorite passages would come to me like the one engraved on the key ring I had used since I turned sixteen: "Those who hope in the Lord will renew their strength. They will soar on wings like eagles; they will run and not grow weary, they will walk and not be faint" (Isaiah 40:31 NIV).

I needed my strength renewed. Psalm 23 says that the Lord is my Shepherd and will take care of me—everything I need—even in the valley of the shadow of death. I remembered Proverbs 3:5–6, which told me that I needed to trust God with all my heart and not depend on my understanding. Singing had always been one of my favorite things, and hymns and choruses would come back to me at random times, many of them almost word for word from God's Word. I remembered a chorus created from Psalm 27:14 (KJV): "Wait on the LORD: be of good courage, and he shall strengthen thine heart: wait, I say, on the LORD." I needed my heart to be strengthened, but it was so very hard to wait, rest, hope, trust, and expect when the present was so full of pain.

A week had passed; it was again time to go to the operating theater for my fourth ten-hour operation in the almost five weeks I had spent in the burn unit. That time I would be grafted with skin taken from my own donor sites. The hurt I felt as I again surfaced from unconsciousness was impossible to bear. I was moaning and thrashing about. I remember being restrained and the nurses trying to reason with me. The pain was excruciating. The smell was more awful than usual. There were lamps on both sides under the sheets shining on my thighs. I stopped thrashing as I entered into reason, but I could not stop moaning and crying. The pain was unbearable. It altered forever how I measure pain.

I was administered a little morphine but to no avail, so I was given more in two-unit increments, I think milligrams. I was up to four. My moaning turned to whimpering. I have no concept of the time that went by before one of my favorite nurses came in and said, "This is ridiculous!" She came back with four more units of morphine, and I blessed her as I mercifully drifted out of consciousness into a fitful sleep.

I thought I saw Dr. H sitting with crossed legs in a chair near the end of my bed. When I woke up again, Dr. H was still there bent over with head in hands, horn-rimmed glasses on his head, but I drifted off again. I would have chalked up my seeing him to the morphine except for the fact that when I was truly awake again, the chair was still there. My parents later told me that he had barely spoken after surgery this time saying that it was a terrible thing to have to do to a young person.

My donor sites felt like road rash combined with a horrific sunburn. Looking at it made it worse; the bloody yellow canvas material over the donor sites was still weeping and stuck to anything that touched it. I tried to be as still as possible. I had two heat lamps over my thighs to dry the donor sites as my body tried to heal by oozing. The smell nauseated me. This was my final surgery before I could supposedly get on with my life.

First, I had to recover, and it took every fiber of my being to focus my mind. I could not take even a small step into the darkness of the pain or I would lose any control I had over myself. I already felt I had lost control of my mind. I know that God allowed me to look into that abyss and face it while He held me. Facing that place, coming so close that I could see, hear, and feel its despair and madness fundamentally changed me and left scars in places no human eye can see.

People have told me that I was strong. I'd like to think that I am, but I think *stubborn* might be the more appropriate word. "You're a fighter." I think that's the same song, second verse. But I came far too close to the edge to be able to hold myself back. I know I had no strength left to resist. Prayers and God's Spirit held my mind and spirit intact. I guess the emptiness in my eyes prompted those around me to keep bringing up the positives.

I had both hands and both knees. When I went up to the rehab floor, I would have my own room. I would be in a wheelchair soon. When anyone came in my curtained space, I smiled politely and asked questions about nothing to appear normal so that I would be left alone as soon as possible and to feel as little as possible.

When the donor sites were mostly dry, the rehab doctors were brought in to consult and prepare for the transition from the burn unit to the rehab unit. I met the man who would make my prosthetic limbs. There were low voices, some poking and prodding, and lots of diagrams, writing, and picture taking. I had lost muscle tone and flexibility in my joints because I had been lying nearly flat if not completely flat for over two months. My nerve endings had been dulled in my remaining fingers. They did not feel hot, cold, dull, or sharp, but my palms felt like they had pins and needles in them. My stumps had phantom pains that came and went along with random, painful, and seemingly electric shocks that would make me jerk uncontrollably. The rest of my extremities were a patchwork of normal and damaged sensations. I had a physical therapist on and off throughout my time in the burn unit who would visit me as often as possible to move my limbs. He was able to work with my fingers and arms trying to make them mobile.

The next step was to sit up a little higher and longer each day. This new daily routine was a kinder, less-invasive form of torture/therapy that replaced the debridement sessions. Little Anna had been discharged before my last surgery, but I thought of her as the pink, elephant-nose feeding tube was removed (gag in reverse). So began the adventure of relearning to feed myself, which required my total concentration. If for some reason I looked away from what I was holding in my hand, I ended up wearing it.

The day came when I was placed in a big, blue cardiac chair, a transportation chair that was padded and reclined incrementally. I had to sit in it for ten minutes. It was unpleasant and made me feel sick; I was not even close to sitting up straight. As soon as I hit an hour of tolerating sitting, a short outing was planned to get me away from the hospital environment for an hour. They put me in my mom's prepared car to drive me around to a park for lunch and to breathe the fresh autumn air. It was so bright outside that my eyes hurt. My mom bought me a hamburger and fries and drove me to a park overlooking the lake. It was both beautiful and disheartening. The sparkling water, the sensations, and the smell of the outdoors were like life itself. I heard some college students laughing as they walked to the lake and thought, *That should be me.* It was like being slapped by another dose of reality. I smiled, but I couldn't wait to get back to my dark, isolated bed in the hospital. Once back there, I feigned sleep so I could cry alone.

The big blue chair slowly became more like an armchair than a recliner. The canvas scabs over my donor sites peeled off to reveal bright-pink scars. The holes in the grafted skin slowly filled in, and my deep hole, that mine shaft, was requiring only one piece of gauze to fill it in.

Two weeks after the last surgery, I was in a wheelchair though I was too weak to push it myself. I was getting ready to leave the burn unit and be transferred to the rehab unit. My stumps had to be elevated at all times as we toured the hospital. I lived in fear of bumping my stumps into someone or something. I became painfully aware of the way people looked at me or avoided looking at all as we ventured out of the burn unit.

Physical and occupational therapy intensified. Because I could then sit up, I was being trained to do my own wound care. A few spots were just refusing to heal. Most of the little spots were my skin being overzealous in trying to heal and producing excess tissue, keloid tissue. There still remained one more serious and stubborn spot over my patella tendon below my right kneecap. The doctors had explained that wounds heal from the bottom up; they explained it using the correct verbiage, but that's the basic idea. Since this wound had no bottom or underlying dermis to heal from, the healing would happen as the skin graft adhered to the surrounding areas and then would slowly heal from the sides, which was a slow process. Until then, I had to maintain cleanliness and moisture on that place. Making my remaining fingers work was difficult enough when I tried to feed myself let alone remove a sterile, Vaseline-soaked gauze pad from its foil packaging. I was far from doing anything independently, but I needed to know how to do what had to be done.

Just as I was getting used to my hands without bandages, the first of my Jobst garments arrived for my hands and wrists. Jobst manufactures custom compression garments designed to reduce scarring especially from keloid and hypertrophic scar tissue. These long, flesh-colored gloves that closed with zippers were impossible to put on independently and were their own kind of torture. They were to be worn twenty-three hours a day seven days a week for six to twelve months. They are tight enough that blistering is a common side effect during the first two or three weeks. I was waiting for the others to arrive: one for each stump and then a bike short version that came up about four inches above my waist. The bike short version had a cutout for body functions since they were to be removed only once a day for wound care. Zippers were on each of them, and the cloth flaps needed to be perfectly placed.

I know they were designed to help, but they were their own kind of torture; ask any burn patient. I have wondered if any studies have been done on their effectiveness on emotional scarring as well because you get so consumed with how incredibly uncomfortable the Jobst things are that you don't have the opportunity to think about the hell you went through in the burn unit. When we burn patients met, we inevitably got around to complaining about the Jobst garments especially when we were still wearing them.

Before officially being discharged from the burn unit in early October, Dr. H and yet another new resident examined my wounds and scars and pulled the long, white Hickman catheter out of my chest. The nurses helped me wrangle into all the Jobst garments, and I was transported up three floors to the rehab unit. This might sound strange, but I wasn't overly excited about leaving the burn unit. A few of the burn nurses I considered more as friends; I would miss them and their daily support. I had been safely hidden away in my dark corner in the burn unit not exposed to the world. I was afraid of the unknown. That was not the face I wore, but it was in my heart.

"I know the plans I have for you …" but I wasn't sure I did. I certainly didn't like the way the plan was shaping up so far. I knew that if God existed, and I believed He did, He could do whatever He did without my permission and I needed to make the best of it. As one of my burn nurses was taking me up to my new room, I held my chin up and acted brave telling myself, *I am strong; I'm a fighter* as I warily watched anyone who got within two feet of my protruding stumps, which was everyone in the elevator. The elevator doors opened to a sunlit foyer that connected two units. We had barely exited when something bumped into my wheelchair—a remote-controlled car. I looked around and saw two ten-year-old boys snickering in their chairs by the window. The rehab unit was next to the pediatric unit. *Boys will be boys*, I thought as the nurse said something to them. I half-smiled in spite of myself.

I saw that they had the white tubes tucked into their shirt pockets; the whites of their eyes and skin had that telltale yellowish hue topped with hair that was far too thin for kids that young. I heard the little car and their laughter behind us as we moved toward the nurses' station. The boys were trying to hold on to life as death came closer. I was reminded and not for the last time that some people were in situations much more difficult than mine. I had escaped my close encounter with death and had to relearn how to live.

Two really good things happened upon my arrival in the rehab unit. First of all, I got to wear clothes, real clothes like underwear for the first time in nearly three months. I looked comfortable even though the Jobsts were uncomfortable. The second was just as good. I was able to sit to go to the bathroom. Go ahead and laugh, but when you have used a bedpan for as long as I did, you would have been thankful too even with the Jobsts.

I could not dress or go to the bathroom independently. Having someone else dress you is humiliating, and having someone undress you and then lift you onto the shower/bathroom wheelchair is equally humbling, but I was able to sit up by myself at that point. The difference between a shower chair and a bathroom chair was the bucket under the bathroom chair; it was basically a toilet seat on wheels.

I'd be covered from neck to legs with a white warming blanket and then wheeled out and down the hallway to the shower room. There is a slight flaw to this system; one's backside is completely exposed. The draft as one is wheeled down the hallway is a constant reminder of this exposure even though you may be quite toasty under the blanket. I strengthened my ability to grip by holding on to that blanket for all I was worth. Inevitably, I would meet fellow patients in the hallway most of whom were male who may or may not have been in the same blanket-covered situation.

Many times, there was a short queue for the shower room, so there we were making small talk while feeling more exposed than covered. But it was glorious under the shower. After the first week, I was washing myself mostly. I still needed help washing my hair. I ended up going last when I was on the shower schedule; I loved taking long showers, but I think they used my hair-washing attempts as therapy. I kept going until my arms were shaking with fatigue and I couldn't hold them up any longer.

Life on the rehab floor was predictably unpredictable. We were a combination of spinal cord injuries, brain injuries due to trauma or stroke, and other—my category. Everyone received a daily schedule of events Monday through Friday. It was like school in some ways. The nurses got us ready and moved us out to the nurses' station for pickup by the transport people. We had to be waiting in place at the appropriate time, which was the scariest part of my day given my extreme anxiety about my outstretched stumps being bumped.

Our schedules were staggered so the nurses could attend to all of us. The transport person would take two or three of us at a time down the elevator to the rehab area, which served inpatients and outpatients alike. Most of us had physical therapy (PT) two or even three times a day, occupational therapy (OT) once or twice, recreational therapy (RT) once a day plus extras—parties, field trips, movies, consults with the rehab doctor team, vocational therapy, individual rehabilitative counseling with a psychologist, and support groups two to three times a week. Those were the predictable parts of the equation. However, the mixture of patients made for certain adventures and ample opportunity for things to not quite go according to plan; hence the unpredictable part.

In the burn unit, my therapist had done as much PT and OT with me as possible. He was also a Christian and often prayed with and encouraged me. He was one of the people whom God sent as a ministering angel. He visited me in rehab during my first week, but then new therapists took over my care.

In PT, the first goal was to increase my strength and mobility, range of motion, so I could transfer in and out of a wheelchair by myself. Every time I came down to PT, the wooden plank, a strange skateboard without wheels, was pulled out. The transfer board bridged the gap between the wheelchair and whatever surface I was trying to get to, in my case, some raised exercise mats. Though I could not move myself at all, I began to be lifted in the way that I would eventually transfer myself.

I was then given pathetically easy exercises that were nonetheless impossible for me to complete on my own. For instance, I had to bench press a wooden dowel like a broom handle ten times. By three, I was shaking and sweating. By five reps, I needed help to stabilize the weight of the dowel or it would dip me off center. By seven, my rat claw could not hold the dowel independently. By nine, I'd be trying not to cry. By ten, I was drenched in sweat and utterly exhausted and discouraged. I did not recognize the body I inhabited. I lay there catching my breath and thinking, *One day, this will all be over.* I was helped back into the sitting position so I could transfer back to the wheelchair.

OT consisted of putting my hands in a machine that blew bits of corn husks around to desensitize my hypersensitive palms and nubs. Then I picked up pieces of different materials and shapes and put them in their appropriate places on a board while being timed.

The best part of OT was taking off the Jobsts; the worst part was putting them back on.

Then I went to recreational therapy, which was in some ways similar to OT because the board games we played required picking up a piece and moving it with precision. I saw a few familiar faces there. One was one of the boys from the pediatric floor, but his white tube was hooked up to an IV. Another one was the therapist who had visited me when I was in the burn unit. I had to start by apologizing to her. When she had introduced herself back then as the recreational therapist, I was sarcastic to say the least. She had facilitated a TV and VCR (yes, I'm old) for little Anna and me along with a list of movies.

The support group met after lunch; that's where I officially met most of my fellow patients for the first time. I was the anomaly, the other; everyone else had spinal cord injuries. There was one other woman in the group; she was a few years older than I was. She had been riding behind her boyfriend on a motorcycle and had been thrown into a concrete ditch. She was in a halo, a medical apparatus that surrounds the head and is attached to the skull to keep the neck and head immobile as the patient's cervical fusion heals. All she could move were her eyes. The other twenty or so patients were males between ages seventeen and thirty. I said hello, but that was about it because as I looked around and listened, I realized that I was with people for whom it would never be over, whose bodies might not improve. Ever. That was their situation. Deanna (not her real name) said she would have given anything to pick up a spoon and feed herself even if a lot of it never made it to her mouth. I was ashamed of my own self-pity after I left the group. That night, I came up with a whole list of things I was thankful for when I prayed.

My parents and brother were trained in using the transfer board to help me get in and out of the car. One weekend, they came down to visit, and we went out for pizza. It was my first outing. I was just getting settled in my chair in the parking lot when some teenage girls walked by and stared at me. I avoided eye contact, but all of us heard one girl exclaim in disgust, "Oh, *gross!*" I couldn't disagree; that was how I felt. It was a sobering moment. No amount of makeup or designer clothes would mask my disfigured body. I felt relief upon returning to the hospital's rehab floor, where I was safely in the company of people who understood being suddenly different.

I could write a book about what I heard on the rehab floor. After my first week, I was slowly becoming more independent in the wheelchair; a pair of bike gloves helped my grip tremendously and protected my hyper, pins-and-needles palms. Even so, I still needed help from the transport orderlies to get to and from the rehab area. So with my stumps elevated out in front of me, I waited with a group of others in front of the nurses' station. Spinal cord injuries vary in severity, but most of them are identified by the location of the injury—C for cervical or L for lumbar and then the corresponding number of the disk. Based on that, you had a general idea of their limitations. The body is complex and truly amazing besides being individual. For example, Deanna's break was fairly high, a C4, but she could move a finger on her right hand and move a foot.

However, brain trauma is far less predictable. Brain trauma can cause someone to be damaged physically, mentally, or emotionally and in any combination or degree. One such patient was an elderly gentleman who had fallen off his bike headfirst. He was able to walk and talk, but his judgment was severely impaired, and he could not be left alone. He had to relearn the daily activities of life. Virgil (not his real name) was also an escape artist. As we were waiting at the nurses' station one time, the nurse there was called to assist in a room. Virgil saw his chance to run away … with me.

"You're kinda cute. You're comin' with me!" With that, we were off, Virgil pushing me in my wheelchair to the laughter and cheers coming from the spinal cord guys. At that point, my panic level was at DEFCON 1 not because I was afraid we'd get far—Virgil would forget where the bathroom in his own room was—but because I just knew he was going to slam me into a door or wall. So I tried to reason with him to stop. The double doors were quickly approaching as Virgil picked up speed.

"The stairs are faster!" he declared excitedly.

"Virgil, I'm in a wheelchair! I can't do stairs!"

Every muscle in my body braced for impact. For the first time, I noticed a door coming up on the right that had a fire exit sign and an ominous plaque that read Stairs. I wondered how he could remember where the stairwell was but not the rehab area or his own bathroom. "We'll run away later, OK, Virgil?" I was desperate. He was slowing down. He let go of my wheelchair even though we had not come to a stop, and he went to open the door to the stairs. I barely moved out of the way fast enough, and I was so thankful for my bike gloves, which gave me some control over my movement. To my immense relief, there was a foot-high wooden barricade across the doorway to the stairs. Virgil, however, was undeterred as he let go of the door to get me back. Thankfully, another hand took hold of my wheelchair and then took hold of Virgil. The nurse took us back to the nurses' station as the guys booed and congratulated Virgil on the morning's excitement. My motivation to gain independence as quickly as possible was renewed.

Since I could not be independent, my family was brought in to learn how to make our home as accessible as possible and how to get help doing that. They also had to learn to lift and assist me.

My first home visit was scheduled for the first weekend in November. I slowly progressed to the point that I was able to get down to the rehab area and back to my room by myself. I also was to dress myself in bed as putting on pants required a lot of rolling from side to side. The Jobsts actually helped because clothes slid over them. I was also to do my own face washing, teeth brushing, and hair care. However, gaining this independence required a lot of time and effort. I had to wake up earlier, which didn't make me happy as I have never been a morning person. That and how difficult the most basic tasks of personal care could be plus the amazing number of ways things could go awry made for many frustrating moments. I have no idea how many tubes of toothpaste I went through not to mention how many caps from the tubes or hair bands I lost. I still needed help with anything that required a transfer. Many times, I had to wait for my nurse to help me onto the bathroom chair and then off it. The faster I tried to go, the worse things went. My hair was supposed to be in a ponytail, but that had to be redone in OT more times than not.

Oh well, I would strap on my bike gloves and away I would roll ... slowly. The guys would harass me in jest as I made my way all the way down the hall. Mercifully, no one said a word about hair because we all had tremendously bad cases of bed head. Inevitably, they would catch up with me at the elevators with the transport people, who would wait for me to push the elevator button. I had to wheel up so the button was on my right side to be close enough to push it. Sometimes, it took me a couple of attempts.

My mishaps were their entertainment, so I played along no matter how frustrated I was. "After you ..." I would say to them with a slight gesture toward the elevator. I think the transport people took pity on me and allowed me to wait for the next elevator. I would always wave at them as the doors closed and they got in their last comments: "See you this afternoon!" It was eight in the morning. "Don't get lost!" "Watch out for Virgil!"

PT was always the first stop on my schedule every weekday. The first half-hour was dedicated to building up strength, and the last half-hour was dedicated to getting rid of the contractures in my knees and hips. Basically, my knees and hips would not straighten; they were locked in a bent position that would make walking extremely difficult. Extreme stretching was implemented to allow as full a range of motion as possible to make walking more of a possibility. Since I could not straighten my knees or hips on my own, my physical therapists often required the application of their own weight to gain the smallest of increases.

I would be sweating and my hair declared a disaster area before I was on my way to OT. There, we would work on my hair. My occupational therapist would guide my hands and offer suggestions and different techniques for me to try.

I would go to vocational therapy and discuss my plans to finish college. The vocational therapist asked me a lot of questions that irritated me because I kept thinking that those situations didn't apply to me as I would be walking soon. I just couldn't accept that I would need so much assistance; it was easier to live in denial.

Then there were my personal counseling sessions. Madison University Hospital is a teaching hospital, so of course it was me against three—the psychologist and two residents. Their questions upon questions probing my heart and mind felt intrusive and were certainly unwelcome as I was just trying to get through this as best I could without stopping along the way to think about anything more than I had to. My sarcasm was a never-ending dialogue in my head. I sincerely tried to answer the way I was supposed to so I could avoid more sessions, and I sincerely took pride in receiving a report of how well I was adjusting to my new circumstances.

One day, I had had enough and was teetering on the brink of just giving up physically, mentally, emotionally, and spiritually. I decided to go up another set of elevators. It was not the fastest route, so it was the one less traveled. I just wanted to get back to my room while avoiding running into anyone I knew or seeing any of the kids from the pediatric ward and feeling compelled to smile and say something.

Everything was going according to plan when I got out of the elevator. Then I saw that the double doors that separated the lobby from the floor hallways had closed. Normally, these doors were left open during the day, but fire alarms and other alarms caused them to close automatically. If I had gone up the regular elevators, it would not have been a problem because there was so much traffic that someone would have propped them open soon enough.

Though the rehab people wouldn't have opened the door for me because being on my own meant that I was able to work independently and open them myself, one of the kids or his or her family member would have opened them to be nice. Opening a self-closing door by pulling it toward me in a wheelchair was not easy at that point in my recovery. Those fire doors were very heavy. When

I managed to get one open, I was not in the right position to get through the opening. The door would close as I struggled to get my wheelchair in the open space, its weight causing my wheelchair to angle off. My stumps were also propped up in front of me making this process even more difficult.

I had to rest, analyze, problem solve, and start over. I guess I could have gone down the elevator and come up the normal route, but the thought never occurred to me. It took me forty-five exhausting minutes to open that door and get in. I was frustrated and angry to the point of tears. My emotions took over the moment I was safely in my room. Sobbing, I reached for a tissue and knocked my paperback Bible off the bedside table. Miraculously, I caught it by the front cover and was amazingly able to hold on to it and place it on my lap. Through my tears, I read the prayer I had written there just before I had gone to Spain the year before.

> Lord, I give up all my plans and purposes, all my desires and hopes, and accept Thy will for my life. I give myself, my life, my all utterly to Thee to be Thine forever. Fill me and seal me with Thy Holy Spirit. Use me as Thou wilt, send me where Thou wilt, work out my life at any cost, now and forever. Pam

After taking a deep breath, I whispered, "OK, Lord, I guess I asked for it." I felt a probing in my heart asking me, *Do you still trust me?* My angry sobs of broken pride slowly gave way to sobs of surrender and a broken heart as I slowly acknowledged a yes, a broken yes, one full of pain and fear; it was far from a faith-filled, Paul-like yes. Psalm 51:6 confirms that God wants a sincere heart, truth in the inner being, and to teach me wisdom in the hidden places of my heart. God took my feeble yes and filled my heart. Again, I knew that amazing peace of God's presence in that moment. It flooded my mind and soul and left its mark on my memory like the memorial stones in the Old Testament. It was as if God had once again pulled me out of the pit in an event that I would remember as God confirming His presence to me. My circumstances remained the same, however; I was still challenged by toothpaste caps, hair bands, waiting, weakness, and stares.

The first weekend of November finally arrived, and everything had been arranged for me to leave the hospital with the necessary medical equipment for my first home visit. So midmorning that Friday, my parents came to get me. I had my list of things to take: my wound care kit, Ace bandages for my stumps since the Jobsts had become too loose as the swelling had decreased, a bag of dirty clothes, my wheelchair, and myself.

My parents had set up a bed and a toilet chair with a bucket in the downstairs living room since the upstairs bedrooms were an impossibility. They had built a ramp leading to the front door. It was a confusing mix of emotions; anticipation and apprehension of the known and unknown churned in my head and wreaked havoc on my stomach. Pillows were piled under and around me. My stumps were always to be propped up. I was going to be cast for my prosthesis, my artificial legs, the following week, so I was to follow strict instructions to avoid anything that would cause excess swelling.

I watched the fall colors go by on the three-hour ride home. Mom and Dad brought me up to date on the news around town and in the church. I found out that the community was having a benefit dinner for my family hosted by the Catholic church in town.

Greenwood, Wisconsin, had a population of 1,256 in 1988. St. Mary's Catholic Church was the largest church in town. While I was in high school, our school choir had sung in each of the churches in town on Sunday mornings with our repertoire of sacred music. Nobody objected. People know each other in a small town, and news travels fast. I had been in plays, musicals, sports, band, marching band, choir, and swing choir during high school. In a graduating class of fifty-eight, everyone knew everyone, and most of the families knew all the other families. When the school had a sporting, musical, theatrical, or other event, most of the town showed up; we were a tight-knit community. My dad was a clergy member in a community where the clergy met regularly. When I got sick and went to the hospital, it was in the local papers. The fact that I was still in the hospital was common knowledge.

In a town centered around dairy farmers and cheese factory workers, people banded together when someone needed help. A few years earlier, lightning had struck our house and started a fire. The siren in town had sounded, and the volunteer firefighters had all come to our aid. They were just regular people who gave extra time to train and volunteer when farming was a 24/7 job not to mention answering the call every time the siren sounded.

Our community had decided to do something for my family, and St. Mary's was hosting the event for the Baptist preacher's family. It made my heart warm and glad though it was accompanied by a sense of shame and embarrassment that I was the cause of our neediness and the focus of attention for a situation I didn't want to be in.

The parsonage where we lived did not have a wheelchair-accessible bathroom, and my second-floor bedroom was beyond my reach. Since the front door was about thirty-five feet from the church's front door, I worried about too many guests. I worried about their reactions to me. I worried about using the bathroom. The knots in my stomach grew tighter and tighter as we got closer to home. When we finally arrived home and were settled in, I finally relaxed. Mom, Dad, Eric, and I were talking and watching TV. It felt almost normal.

On Saturday, I woke up in the living room and watched life happen around me. Every time I needed something, I had to ask for it, and I knew the burden that put on my mom especially. The thick carpet was much more challenging to navigate than the slick linoleum floors of the hospital had been, but I had no place to go. I couldn't go to the kitchen or anywhere else; my wheelchair simply didn't fit through the doorways. And I was mostly in the way unless I stayed on the bed.

On Sunday, I was rolled to church and greeted kindly. When people were standing, I couldn't see anything but their midsections. When they sat, I towered over them in the wheelchair, so I sat in the back as out of the way as possible. People really tried, but the stares and whispers were impossible to ignore.

The same thing happened when we showed up at the benefit dinner. People tried, but what could they say? I didn't blame them, and I was so touched that the community and the Catholic church would do all this for the Baptist minister's family. When someone gave me something to eat, I parked my wheelchair, took off my bike gloves, and carefully began to eat. A local politician came over and clasped my hand in a handshake. The pencils fell from his other hand; he recovered well, but I knew the exact moment that he had lost his composure if only for a moment. It was when he felt the nub where a finger should have been and he hadn't expected that. I was wearing my Jobsts, but even so, he noticed. I smiled through it all.

Most of my friends were away at college, but I saw some people I had gone to high school with whose eyes wouldn't meet mine. Others tried to encourage me; a classmate told me that she knew exactly how I felt because she had had a badly sprained ankle that had ruined her whole summer. My interior dialogue was screaming, but I smiled through it all. How could I possibly expect anyone to understand what this felt like? At least she had tried.

We went home to gather things before returning to the hospital, but I realized that the world outside the hospital was going to be a place I would no longer fit into. I mean, if I had thought I hadn't fit in before and that no one had really understood me, the new me was all that times ten—maybe times a hundred or even a thousand. I decided it was the end of any future I had thought or dreamed of. It was time to accept that fact.

Before leaving for the hospital that Sunday afternoon, I carefully wrote a short note to Antonio and put it in the packing envelope already addressed to him. I told him he needed to be free. I did not want him to stay with me out of pity. He spoke continually of a future for us that I just couldn't see. The future was an ominous, unknown darkness. I didn't think he understood and was living in even more denial than I was. How could he understand? I was having a hard time recognizing myself. I told him that I did not want to hurt him and that this was the right thing to do to avoid hurting him further. I told him that I knew I had loved him, but at the time, I felt nothing. I was numb. I told him that's how it was in general, that I just wanted to be alone. I told him not to call or write me because I would not answer. I did not think it was fair to wait and see how things turned out. A clean break was best. I thanked him for everything and wished him the best. I took a last look at his ring before I slipped it in the envelope and sealed it. I left it on the small stack of outgoing mail near the front door.

We listened to music on the way back to Madison University Hospital. I did my best not to think about anything. The closer we got to the hospital, the more I relaxed. I belonged at the hospital; I no longer belonged in the rest of the world. I felt more foreign in the house, the church, and the town I had lived in for the past seven years than I had ever felt in a foreign country where I had looked and sounded out of place. Back at the hospital, I settled in my bed, put on my Walkman, and drifted to sleep without allowing my heart to interact with the thoughts in my head. It was too much to even allow tears to fall.

My prosthetist came again the following week. I had regained enough flexibility and strength to begin the process of being fitting for artificial legs. I had some questions; I wanted to know if I could change my shoe size. He said yes; he said a smaller size would actually be beneficial. Having worn size tens since junior high, I was thrilled about that change; I thought that maybe I could finally wear some cool shoes. My priorities were sort of messed up, but I was taking any happy thought I could find.

"Size eight?" I asked tentatively.

"Sounds good," he said matter-of-factly.

I dared to dream bigger. "Can I be shorter?"

"It depends on you, but height is better."

"I would really like to be five-eight; then my pants would fit."

If you were a tall teen in the eighties in rural Wisconsin, no pair of women's jeans would ever be long enough, and after I got my prosthetic legs, I wanted long jeans. He just smiled and wanted to take a look at my stumps. He palpated all over the surface of my stumps as I clenched my teeth and dug what fingernails I had into the mat, but every so often, a little yelp escaped. His happy manner turned solemn as he asked my physical therapist to feel the end of my right stump.

She nodded. "We have to check that out." She left.

My prosthetist explained that it felt as if I had a bone spur that would have to be removed and I would have to be completely healed before I could be fitted for the prosthetics. He returned with a rehab doctor and a resident who felt the end of my stump as I bit back tears due to the discomfort and for the realization that I would more than likely be facing another surgery. The X-rays confirmed what everyone had felt; it looked like a little finger was growing out of the end of my tibia. Surgery was set for the following Monday so I could go home over the weekend.

Dr. H was called in, and he as usual looked at my hands and nodded while mumbling, "That's good, good … Looks good." That was his way of saying hello. Then he started checking all my grafts and squeezing some of them. He explained that since we had to operate anyway, they would make the most of it and do some revisions on some of the grafted areas. I was just too bummed about the whole surgery thing to even care. My attitude was, *Do whatever you have to do.* The only point I wanted to make was that if my left stump had a bone spur, do that one too. They told me the left one was fine.

On Friday, my mom made the three-hour trip to Madison. We loaded my dirty clothes, medical supplies, wheelchair, and me into the car and started for home. I have always loved the fall. The trees had all changed; many were more than half-bare as they stood against the darkening grey sky. I loved the smell of burning leaves. The cornfields of chopped-off pale-yellow stems in straight rows were waiting for that first snow. Looking out the window had become a balm for my soul. My mind wandered in the silent spaces between conversations. Memories and random thoughts changed as fluidly as the landscapes that we traveled did. So did my silent prayers of thanks, wonder, and yes, fear and doubt as well. I realized that I saw much more than I had noticed before. It was all there, but I hadn't seen or appreciated the details of the world that surrounded me as much as I did then. I knew all the hills, marshes, ponds, and rivers along that road home.

I also knew where every possible safe (as I called them) bathroom was. McDonald's was the most recognizable safe place because most of their bathrooms were big and accessible even in the days before 1990, when the Americans with Disabilities Act mandated changes to make public places accessible to the growing number of disabled persons in the United States. I could not make it home without at least one stop and maybe two, and it took time to unpack the wheelchair, get the transfer board in place, transfer to the wheelchair, get to the bathroom, adjust clothing, transfer to the toilet, and then doing all that in reverse; it took energy as well as time even though my mother helped me.

One of my priorities was to be able to use a bathroom by myself, and part of my rehab experience was to use the stalls in the hospital's visitors' bathroom. I was doing much better, but I could not maneuver the wheelchair and be able to turn around and close the door. I still needed some help getting my pants up all the way too unless we wanted to tack on an additional fifteen minutes to the experience. My visit home was just another reminder that I had to keep working on becoming independent. My present limitations were difficult for everyone, but when I left the hospital for good, I would be ready for independence.

"Ten, nine, eight …" I wanted to throw up. I had to throw up. As I turned to heave, a nurse was right there to help me in the recovery room. My throat was in agony. This operation had taken only five hours, but throwing up through a throat made raw by a recently removed breathing tube is the worst. Thank goodness my stomach was empty. I couldn't drink anything yet, so they let me just wash my mouth out. The nausea wasn't letting up. It felt like forever, but Dr. H's resident appeared with a shot of some kind to help stop the upheaval I was experiencing. As he stuck a syringe in a good skin area of my hip, he explained that this was a reaction to the anesthesia after so many long surgeries. He said I would be taken to a room where a machine would focus radiation on my stump to prevent the bone from growing back. Apparently, it was much like keloid tissue in that the fragmented bone was being overzealous in its attempt to heal.

When the gurney moved, I felt the guillotine pain in my stump and bit the inside of my mouth to stop from screaming. Who knew there were so many bumps on a linoleum floor? I was wheeled into a room that was all machine except for a small platform in the middle. There was a debate about how to do this as I was no longer groggy, which I guessed had been the original plan—to do this while I was groggy. I was lifted onto the platform, and the machine moved around me. The pain involved in that transfer was intense. The good thing was that I was alone and could cry in peace with the huge radiation machine thing. No one said anything to me, and I certainly did not need any encouragement to stay still, so my illusion of solitude was unbroken.

Finally, back in my room and dosed up on morphine, I slept rather fitfully. The nausea did not go away, so I barely ate or drank anything. The next morning, the pediatric nurse slipped over to my floor to draw my blood as usual at 5:30. My veins were proving elusive even to her. One of my burn unit nurses came up to check on my sutures and drains, and between the two of them, they found a vein that would allow poking. Shortly after, I heard an exhale, like a sigh, as she unwrapped my stump. I started paying attention and started looking for something hideous, but I saw just a scraped-up, scabby area on the graft at my knee. I had fought against the surgical dressing to bend my knees in my sleep, and the bandages had sluffed away part of the graft. Sutures and drains were fine with wounds healing nicely, but everyone seemed to focus on that graft. I had three more days of radiation treatments, but my pain levels subsided quickly, and I was able to be transported in my wheelchair. After the drains and stitches were out, my daily schedule resumed.

I was met by my doctors and residents and my prosthetist and physical therapist at my mat in the PT gym. They basically informed me that on Wednesday of the following week, the day before Thanksgiving, I would be discharged until the first week of January. They told me that I had made a lot of progress and would soon recover my strength and gain confidence with the wheelchair. I would have to continue stretching PT at a clinic twenty miles from my house to minimize the contractures in my knees as much as possible before my return.

My prosthetist explained that if my graft could not take the pressure of a bandage, it would not withstand the pressure of my weight bearing down on a prosthetic leg. So these weeks of holidays would be a time for me to get out of the hospital and heal. He winked at me and told me to bring those size eight shoes before I left. My parents also received instructions.

The time between that moment and going home was disquieting for many reasons. I was disappointed to go home in a wheelchair for over a month. I had thought that I would walk out of that hospital and pick up at least some part of my life. My parents had been continually pressed by the hospital home liaisons to create a wheelchair-accessible bedroom and bathroom, but our home belonged to the church. Blueprints had been drawn up and agreed on, but the work had not started. My parents were again pressed to make or find a place where I could be independent in my wheelchair for their sakes and mine. It was out of my parents' hands. I could not imagine being stuck in the living room for six weeks. The thought of the bathroom bucket in the living room made me feel sick to my stomach, and there would be no showers; it was back to bed baths and dirty hair. I had not lived at home for more than two weeks of my previous two years. I relished my independence, so the prospect of being so dependent on my parents and cut off from ... well, life, was not an appealing prospect.

I had, though, improved tremendously from my first days in rehab. I had gained a certain degree of independence at the hospital at least. I didn't spend a lot of time in my room, and I wasn't expected to. Outside my schedule, I could visit anyone anywhere in the hospital or simply go exploring for a different view. I discovered the basement hallways that the staff used to get to stairwells and elevators that were not used by the public. I found them by following the signs to a twenty-four-hour snack bar down an elevator, but I noticed that while visitors just hopped back on the elevator, most of the hospital personnel there had appeared from around corners, so I decided to check them out.

It seems almost absurd now, but it wasn't then. The ability to move at will to wherever I wanted to roll gave me a taste of something resembling control. The nurses on our floor would greet me on their way to attending to other patients as I rolled past, but they never questioned where I was off to or coming from. I gained confidence and endurance in my wheelchair. I began to look at people and smile. A group of about seven of us constantly bantered back and forth. We learned to smile at each other and laugh at ourselves in public and keep our pain private. We didn't talk about how we felt, but things that annoyed us were the topics of lively conversations.

Five of us had been in the hospital for about the same time but in different areas of the ICU. Strangely, the PT gym had become a place of laughter instead of just pain. We were the only people who could be irreverent enough to mess with each other, and we had given each other our unspoken consent to do that. Anger and bitterness consumed others; their isolation was impenetrable, but in our group, one guy had been an all-state athlete with scholarships in football and baseball. A car accident had left him unable to move anything except his head. His wheelchair was being custom built to hold his six-four body and could be controlled by puffs of air from a straw-like input device. Larry's (not his real name) body was stretched and moved while he worked to improve control over his breathing. His cervical break was so high that he had lost a good deal of his capacity to breathe. He could not yell, sneeze, or cough. He slept with oxygen. In his limited voice, he was always urging Virgil to mischief. At a Halloween party for the rehab in-patients, we bobbed for apples that hung from the ceiling. Larry tried it first and kept on bugging me to try until I did. Since that moment, everyone knew us, and we became friends. I could harass him about blowing a ping pong ball and not spitting on it, and he could ask me if I was "missing" anything to the entertainment of everyone, but we read each other like books. Never did we make offhand remarks, and we handled each other's bad days with care. There was no body language to read, our eyes told us everything we needed to know.

They were my social circle; we were loaded up in vans and taken to the movies, a special swimming pool, or the mall. Thinking about going home was like thinking summer camp would soon be over. I knew that life in the hospital wasn't supposed to last, but going home in my state wasn't what I wanted either.

All too soon, it was time for me to go home. Most everyone who had anywhere to go was going out of the hospital for Thanksgiving. I was not alone in my feelings. Our Thanksgiving party was quiet. The PT gym was full of family and staff exchanging papers full of instructions. Even though we were all adults, we became like children again letting the able-bodied grown-ups do all the talking. Deanna was still wearing the halo device. Our eyes met, and we exchanged subdued half-smile of disheartening encouragement.

CHAPTER 6

Hope Deferred

❦

Leaving the hospital for the holidays prompted a mix of emotions; I would add to my growing awareness of what life in a wheelchair really meant. Thanksgiving had always been a favorite holiday of mine. Going to my aunt and uncle's farm, a three-hour drive from home and only an hour from Green Bay, had always been fun. Time spent with family and cousins was especially something I had looked forward to. We cheered on football games and then went out and played football between the family's Chicago branch and the Wisconsin branch.

My memories made me excited, but then my physical reality would crash down on those happy memories. There would be no visits with the animals, or helping out, or playing football; there would be sitting and being in the way. My stomach twisted in knots as we drove, and I tried to focus out the window.

Thanksgiving was bittersweet, but I smiled and shed tears of gratitude for the reunion with my aunt and uncle and cousins on the farm. They did everything and beyond to make that Thanksgiving weekend as normal and as special for me as they could. They had me spend the night just as I had always done. They let me stay in the master bedroom so I could use the bathroom. We drove to Green Bay, and they wrestled my wheelchair around, and we went shopping at the mall. They flanked me with their love and care. They bought me a winter coat that was stylish and practical for the wheelchair because it was short and could be cinched tight at the wrists and waist. They bought me an expresso coffee maker, which was a big deal then, so I could come home and drink coffee Spanish style. I was the only coffee drinker in my house. I was embarrassed at the lavish gifts and attention, but I was so thankful that they wanted me around. It was the most special and normal I had felt in a long time.

Despite that positive experience, I was anxious about our next plans. We were going to attend my grandmother's funeral; my mom had been dividing her time between Milwaukee and Madison hospitals for the previous two months. After that, the next big trip was to Indiana; we drove the eight hours to my college to pick up my things. It should have been my last year; I had taken every class I could to finish my English degree in three years. The college knew we were coming and had arranged for us to stay in guest faculty housing. They had also arranged for me to speak to the student body in a chapel service. That was making me feel nauseous for a number of reasons, not the least of which was my anxiety about being lifted and carried down a flight of stairs to the chapel and then lifted onto the stage in front of all the students. Speaking there did not frighten me any more than it did anyone else, which is to say I couldn't sleep the night before. The speaking part meant that I would see people and that they would see me, which meant seeing faces familiar and unknown. I was afraid of seeing their reactions. I didn't want anyone's pity, but I didn't want to be rejected either. I just wanted to disappear in the crowd, sit in the back, smile, greet a few people, and leave. My emotions terrified me. How would I react being back at my college? Going to visit the pizza place where I had worked? How would they view me? I had already faced many reactions from people, but I didn't like facing them just the same.

Then, after being up on that platform for everyone to see, I would have to be lifted again in reverse order. I obsessed on that detail. I am not a small person, and I do not like being lifted and having no control. Being completely vulnerable and constantly fearing I would bang my stumps, be pitied, or be rejected made me sick and on the verge of tears.

When we arrived, everything was surreal. It was as if I were visiting the college for the first time. Furtive glances and whispers were all I saw and heard when I looked at passing students for faces I knew. I finally stopped looking anywhere but straight ahead and at the college administrators who accompanied us.

I was shaking badly when the time for chapel came. *What am I doing here? Why am I saying anything?* Self-awareness and doubt crowded in on my prepared speech. I tried not to focus on any face. I summarized what had happened and lifted my hands for everyone to see. There was no point in hiding that. Besides, this public exposure plus the bike gloves might discourage people from wanting to shake my hand later, but my hands were definitely shaking all on their own then.

I shared my favorite verses and a couple of my God experiences, and I thanked them for their prayers. I was so grateful to have God carry me through that experience, and He has done so every time I have spoken publicly since then. Then in an almost slow-motion realization, I saw people standing and applauding, which I didn't understand. *Why are they doing that?* I wondered. But I did not have a choice; those who believe in God have already decided to trust Him. I hadn't chosen my circumstances; I was simply trying to hang on one day at a time in faith, and my heart was raw. I thought that they should applaud relief workers, missionaries, volunteers, and others who did not have to do what they did but chose to do it anyway because their love and compassion compelled them. I was not in that category. I had doubted and struggled; I had not done anything deserving a standing ovation. I felt ashamed.

After chapel, students streamed forward to greet me. I had never spoken with most of them before, but maybe we had shared a class or they had seen me working in the cafeteria. I saw some of my school friends and dorm mates from years past. Some of my professors came to greet me and wish me well. Mostly, I listened and smiled. I was the one who didn't have any idea what to say, but somehow, I bumbled my way through. The people I once felt close to felt distant, as if they belonged somewhere else at that point. Others whom I didn't know felt too close. At the end of the visit, I was physically and emotionally exhausted. I couldn't make any sense of my emotions. I was lost. Being out of the hospital and back in my old world forced issues I had suppressed to bubble up to the surface. I had pushed them down because I had not had enough physical, intellectual, or emotional strength to face anything except what was in front of me at any one moment. And there at college, where I had been so focused on a goal with a plan for my life, I felt empty, lost. Grieving yes, but so angry at what I had lost after I had finally found a sense of identity and a place in this world not long before that.

As we drove home, I realized I had no idea where to begin again. I finally began to understand the questions the vocational therapist had asked me that I had dismissed so quickly. Another level of understanding weighed so heavily on my heart and mind that I could barely breathe. Pain has a way of reaching down and shaking a soul to its core. All the questions that were more easily pushed away into the dark recesses of the mind come out screaming when all life's comforting props have been swept away. I said I believed in God; I had told Him that I trusted Him. Even so, there I was again coming face to face with all those questions and doubts that had been lurking in my heart, mind, and soul; they turned into accusations because Satan, the author of death, knows what lives in the dark and will use it to his advantage.

I was in a dark season of doubt that December. Christmas found me filled with despair. The Christmas tree with its colorful lights and the nativity of baby Jesus in remembrance of Immanuel, God with us, shared the same space with me in the living room 24/7, but a broken spirit is unmoved by pretty trappings and decorations that have no power to heal.

Is my faith a crutch, a way of hiding from reality? Am I brainwashed because I grew up with this belief system? I thought about that long and hard as I stared out the window watching the squirrels attack the bird feeder swaying in the wind from a branch of a pine tree. I had to honestly answer no to both questions. I had tried to give up on God more than once. I thought life would be so much easier if we just simply existed and gave in to … whatever. I confess to even envying those who appeared free from thoughts of a God and especially of the Lord God I believed in who had asked me to put every aspect of my life before Him. My faith required me to think, analyze, and examine the Bible, myself, and the world around me. Perhaps because I have a natural bent toward cynicism and negativity, I had never been able to embrace the "God said it, I believe it, and that's good enough for me" belief. I could give intellectual assent to that statement as being true given that the Bible is what God said, but being headstrong, I seemed to take everything as something to be argued. The flood of emotions and the future implications of my reality were too much for me to process. I could not reconcile these feelings and my faith.

I tried to reason with God about my anger and doubt. In the past, God had met my questions with answers or had simply overwhelmed me with His presence. Other times, like right then, God was silent. I would lie awake in the dark and just mull over the thoughts that bombarded me. I felt like Jonah. I knew God hadn't let me go, but I didn't want to live the life He had left me with. I was angry. It didn't matter if God had a plan or purpose or that I could be a witness for God from my wheelchair to give others hope. I didn't want to be a living object lesson. I didn't ask God why because I believed He had His reasons; instead, I asked Him why He didn't let me die. If God is God, He will do as He pleases without consulting me. I viewed Him not as a loving God but as a tyrant. Since I couldn't run or hide, I resorted to self-pity. I found a verse that became my new theme verse: "Woe to me because of my injury! My wound is incurable! Yet I said to myself, 'This is my sickness, and I must endure it'" (Jeremiah 10:19 NIV).

I add Matthew Henry's commentary here because it sums this

verse up beautifully in its context in Jeremiah. Also, it perfectly conveys the personal application I was assigning to it then even though I would not read his commentary until much later.

> There is no remedy but patience. They cannot help themselves, but must sit still, and abide it: But I said, when I was about to complain of my wound, To what purpose is it to complain? This is a grief, and I must bear it as well as I can. This is the language rather of a sullen than of a gracious submission, of a patience per force, not a patience by principle. When I am in affliction I should say, "This is an evil, and I will bear it, because it is the will of God that I should, because his wisdom has appointed this for me and his grace will make it work for good to me." This is receiving evil at the hand of God, Job 2:10. But to say, "This is an evil, and I must bear it, because I cannot help it," is but a brutal patience, and argues a want [lack] of those good thoughts of God which we should always have, even under our afflictions, saying, not only, God can and will do what he pleases, but, Let him do what he pleases.[4]

I was stuck there in my sullen resignation. I had not wanted to hear or read Romans 8:28 (NIV), "And we know that for those who love God all things work together for good." Hearing or reading that verse caused me to stop listening or reading. Worse still would be if the patience of Job was mentioned. I didn't want to hear it. I did not lie to people when they asked me how I was, but I was certainly not a hundred percent truthful. To the best of my ability, I kept to what I believed in my head and tried to keep the darkness I felt roiling my heart confined. It was better yet to feel nothing at all; I tried my best, after all, "I must bear it as well as I can."

I had excitedly figured out a new trick for putting my pants on after spending so much time in bed in the living room. I would lie on my back and pull my pants on above my knees. I then would roll over so I was prone. Putting most of my weight on my head and hands, I almost got myself kneeling, and from there, I transferred weight to the top of my head while my hands found the waistband and pulled my pants up. I experienced many failed attempts and sideways crashes, but boredom and distractions led me to some discoveries by thinking outside the box.

Here are the facts. People can sit for only so long in wheelchairs even with pressure-relieving cushions before they develop bed sores. Because I had lost sensation in large patches of my posterior not to mention the chunks that were actually missing, I had to contend with bed sores. This meant changing positions at certain intervals. One of my most exciting accomplishments was learning to get down on the floor independently and then get back up in my wheelchair … with a little help.

We went to the PT clinic twice a week. The therapist was an older army guy who terrified me. His goal was to toughen me up. He would smack my stumps with his palm to desensitize them. My nerves were completely frazzled by the time I left. One time, he told me I should be able to jump off a table and land on my stumps. I think he must have realized that I was completely alarmed because he put his hands on my shoulders and told me we weren't going to be attempting that in the next couple of weeks, but he reiterated that we were going to toughen me up. He punctuated that with a hearty pat on both shoulders simultaneously. He worked those contractures in my knees until we were sweating buckets, but he was careful not to displace my kneecaps or endanger my grafts.

The therapist did toughen me up even if it wasn't in the way he was thinking. I realized I was already messed up and knew what pain was, so what did I have to lose by trying new things? Falling would not kill me, and I found out I wasn't as fragile as I had thought. I had also replaced my fear of someone bumping into my stumps with going to see this therapist.

I did not jump down and walk on my stumps (still don't), but slowly and surely, I started kneeling on my bed and on cushions. Putting on pants was no longer a ten-minute ordeal. I also learned that it was much easier to transfer in and out of the wheelchair when kneeling. I would step with my femur from the wheelchair into the car seat and hug the back of the car seat. I would kneel on the car seat and sit from there. That way, I didn't need to drag along the transfer board. Yeah! There was a second motivating factor to this approach; if I transferred the traditional way, my backside would get wet and dirty from sliding across the wheelchair wheels if it had snowed or rained.

My dad had found a car for me, a new car, a blue car. It was beautiful. It was independence day! The dealership sold the car to me at cost, and the hand controls and their installation were free. I could buy this car with a little Christmas help from my parents; my disability checks covered the monthly payments. My dad drove it to a big, snow-covered parking lot, and then I drove it. The hand controls were basically a series of levers that allowed me to manually push down the gas and brake pads with my left hand. I would push the lever down toward the floorboards for the gas pedal and push in toward the dashboard to brake. I had driven a stick shift before, so my stumps instinctively kept reaching for the gas and clutch pedals and I kept wanting to shift. We had a good laugh about that, but the hand controls were easy enough, and with an automatic transmission, there was nothing to it. I drove the whole forty-five-minutes home all smiles, and I drove us wherever after that. I could drive!

However, I was still doing everything in the living room. My mom still had to wait on me hand and foot including handling the dreaded bucket. As happy as I was for my new, beautiful, blue car, as soon as I parked it, it just sat there looking good. It didn't bring me identity, purpose, people, or love. It didn't help me sleep or bring me peace. It was a prop to help me live like I was; it was a fancier wheelchair. A car can't heal the broken places either; I could just pose in it, but inside, I was still lost.

One day at home, I sat on the living room floor unpacking boxes of my college things. The medications that had been used those first couple of weeks in the ICU had adversely affected my memory of the six months before I had gotten sick. I had no recollection of some events, pictures, and papers I had obviously written, which was disconcerting. Then I came to a folder from my freshman composition 101 class that I recalled in its entirety. It was titled, "Life Wasn't Fair." I had meant that God had not been fair with me. After weeks of silence, I felt as if God had handed me that paper and was smiling. His eyes were twinkling because there I was not able to hear or read anything about Job as I held a paper I had written about Job. I rolled my eyes. My nineteen-year-old self read the words that my seventeen-year-old self had penned what seemed a lifetime ago.

Basically, I whined about all the things I had loved and lost. The moves we had made to different places and circumstances, the fact that life consisted of constant change that included gains and losses, and I had blamed the moves for how I felt. The bottom line was that I didn't like myself very much. I laughed at myself as I read it because all those things were minor inconveniences in comparison to my present situation.

However, another thought came into my head. My pain in this paper had been very real, every bit as real as the pain I was experiencing in the present, but my perspective on it had changed. I became more aware with every word I read that these were issues I had not fully resolved. I had written honestly about my struggle with God and the apparent unfairness of how even Jesus treated Peter and John. I put myself in Peter's place and imagined watching Jesus and "the disciple whom Jesus loved," John, spending time together. Jesus never spoke to John the way he did to Peter. It came as no surprise to me that Peter would ask in John 21:21 (NIV), "Lord, what about him?" It was not lost on me that John was the one who had written this. "Jesus answered, 'If I want him to remain alive until I return, what is that to you? You must follow me'" (John 21:22 NIV). I would love to know what tone of voice Jesus used when He said that to Peter, but Peter did what Jesus asked of him. In Acts, Luke recorded Peter and John together though Peter did most of the talking. Through it all, Peter stayed faithful to Jesus Christ and ultimately died a painful death for his belief and for speaking boldly about salvation by faith through Jesus.

I was missing Peter's conviction of two elements: that Jesus was the Christ, the Son of the Living God, the Messiah, and that Jesus/God loved him. Peter did not doubt God's love or goodness, but there I was doubting both.

Then I read what I had written about Job, words that slid off my tongue in songs and as clichés, but my understanding of Job's faith and resolve in the middle of his struggle to understand came alive for me. After receiving bad news piled on bad news after bad news and then heartbreaking news, Job's response was amazing.

> At this, Job got up and tore his robe and shaved his head. Then he fell to the ground in worship and said: "Naked I came from my mother's womb, and naked I will depart. The Lord gave and the Lord has taken away; may the name of the Lord be praised." In all this, Job did not sin by charging God with wrongdoing. (Job 1:20–22 NIV)

As the book progresses, Satan was not content to let Job be because he still had his health, so God allowed him to afflict Job just short of killing him.

> So Satan went out from the presence of the Lord and afflicted Job with painful sores from the soles of his feet to the crown of his head. Then Job took a piece of broken pottery and scraped himself with it as he sat among the ashes. His wife said to him, "Are

you still maintaining your integrity? Curse God and die!" He replied, "You are talking like a foolish woman. Shall we accept good from God, and not trouble?" In all this, Job did not sin in what he said. (Job 2:7–10 NIV)

In all this, Job did not sin with his lips; his integrity held. Just as his wife left, his friends arrived. For seven days, they were excellent friends as ancient custom dictated, but for seven days, they must have been thinking up what they were going to say because thirty-six chapters were dedicated to their long speeches back and forth as Job held firm, and they speculated with authority about why God had done this to Job.

Job defended God and himself, but he did not understand; he had serious, heartfelt questions. He often began answering his friends, but you can almost see him bow his head as he inquired of God Himself. It was as if at some point during his soliloquy, Job forgot that his friends were even there or had already judged that their opinions were not helpful, so he directed his words to God. Job turned to the only One who could possibly help him by fervently seeking Him because Job believed that God had the answers. Job honestly bared his hurting heart to God. His friends were just antagonizing witnesses.

So many people had suggested I read Job for the same reason I had written that paper on him. These millennia-old words from the Bible still provide comfort when our souls are so troubled that we can barely breathe. We are encouraged to freely take our questions and pain to the Lord as well. Job's feeling was mine too: "I loathe my very life; therefore I will give free rein to my complaint and speak out in the bitterness of my soul" (Job 10:1 NIV).

Job believed that God saw and knew everything; He was not like man. God knew Job's heart just as certainly as He knew mine. Job had faith that God made him and that God held him in His hand. No one but God had the ability to save him from his affliction. Even though in one breath Job hated his life, he recognized life, faithful love, and protection of his spirit came from God. Job trusted that He knew why and had His purpose in mind.

I wrote about that observation in Peter. I reflected on how God required others to undergo difficult trials. What held their faith in place was not their fear of God but their faith in His love. My head comprehended those words, but my heart and spirit still could not seem to reconcile this.

Job's replies to his friends continued, and this same pattern reemerged. In Job 13:15, he assured his friends that though God might kill him, he would still trust God because he knew that then he would stand before God, the judge of all, and hear His verdict on his life.

> I know that my redeemer lives, and that in the end he will stand on the earth. And after my skin has been destroyed, yet in my flesh I will see God; I myself will see him with my own eyes—I, and not another. How my heart yearns within me! (Job 19:25–27 NIV)

Job was talking about that final judgment, the time when we also will stand before our Redeemer, Jesus Christ, here on earth regardless of when our bodies of dust die. Just like Job, we will see God with our eyes. I had to admit Job's amazing faith was intertwined with an amazing struggle.

The part of my paper that hit me hardest was the chapters in which God answered Job from the whirlwind. Chapters 38–42 in Job record mostly what God said to him. God the Creator asked, "Who is this that darkens counsel by words without knowledge?" In other words, "Why are you judging me when you have no idea what you're talking about?" Two chapters later, Job got a chance to respond, and I wish I had such a good response. The Lord asked Job,

"Will the one who contends with the Almighty correct him? Let him who accuses God answer him!" Then Job answered the Lord: "I am unworthy— how can I reply to you? I put my hand over my mouth. I spoke once, but I have no answer—twice, but I will say no more." (Job 40:1–5 NIV)

I empathize with Job's answer. I hate conflict. Duck your head down before God and acquiesce. You know, "Humble yourselves before the Lord, and he will lift you up" (James 4:10 NIV). I thought, *Good answer, Job.* But God doesn't take our words at face value; He sees our hearts. He knows us more intimately than we know ourselves, and He understands the depths and layers of our motivation.

Then the Lord spoke to Job out of the storm: "Brace yourself like a man; I will question you, and you shall answer me. Would you discredit my justice? *Would you condemn me to justify yourself?*" (Job 40:6–8 NIV; emphasis mine)

That verse leaped off my paper and pierced my heart. A punch to the stomach would have had less effect. God didn't want Job to stop talking; He didn't want him to just say in resignation, "You're right, God. I don't get it. You are God and I am not. So do whatever." The problem of surrendering, letting go, just to stop the conflict is that the darkness remains in our hearts. Doubt, the poison released in the Garden of Eden, seeps in. Can I see His mighty power? Yes. But do I doubt His love, intentions, and goodness?

Poison a relationship with doubt, and trust is the first casualty. Without trust, love fails. (See 1 Corinthians 13:7.) Self-sustaining allegiance and duty is not what God wanted for or from His creation. He has always desired a relationship based on love and trust. Our

God is a God of mercy; He wants to bring us into an intimate relationship with Him; nothing less is His best plan for us.

I had allowed that poison to infiltrate far beyond what anyone but God could see. He saw me on the living room floor and had prepared this moment for me years before. Amazing grace, that saved a wretch like me. He did so once for salvation, but He continues to extend that grace and mercy.

In Job, God spoke for another two chapters before Job spoke again to God.

I know that you can do all things; no purpose of yours can be thwarted. You asked, "Who is this that obscures my plans without knowledge?" Surely I spoke of things I did not understand, things too wonderful for me to know. You said, "Listen now, and I will speak; I will question you, and you shall answer me." My ears had heard of you *but now my eyes have seen you.* Therefore I despise myself and repent in dust and ashes. (Job 42:1–6 NIV; emphasis mine)

I sat guilty as charged on the living room floor and wept bitterly. Job's questions were never answered, and they remain unanswered. The questions are heard, the tears are stored in a bottle (Psalm 56:8), and at an unexpected moment, God Himself shows up and it is too much to handle. He shows up to correct and comfort.

Job's friends tried to lecture him about the answers to his questions. Job questioned God because he didn't understand why, and he was in tremendous pain in mind, body, and soul. He questioned God because He alone had the answers. Job's friends were posers; they were pretending to have all the wisdom of God. Our Lord doesn't have any patience for religious know-it-alls, but He demonstrates great grace to those who seek Him even when there is struggle in the seeking. Throughout the Bible and in my own experience, seeking and struggling mix more often than not. I remembered those verses that had comforted me months before.

"For I know the plans I have for you," declares the Lord, "plans to prosper you and not to harm you, plans to give you hope and a future. Then you will call on me and come and pray to me, and I will listen to you. You will seek me and find me when you seek me with all your heart." (Jeremiah 29:11– 13 NIV)

I would love to say that Christmas 1988 marked this remarkable turning point in my attitude and faith. It was remarkable because I knew that God had ordained that appointment with Him on the living room floor. It was a turning point in that it checked my angry, bitter heart and humbled me so that I came and prayed to Him, and I know He heard me.

The celebrations of the season were familiar. I sang specials in church from time to time as I always had but on a limited basis. The repeated pressure of tubes in my throat had left my voice true to pitch but gravelly and greatly reduced in range and tone. I don't remember exactly when I found Deniece Williams's song or when my parents purchased the soundtrack on a cassette tape (days before the internet). But as so often happened with me, words from songs and hymns would come to my mind as prayers. This song became my prayer.

My Soul Desire[5]
Chorus: [This reminded me of the prayer I had written in my Bible.]
My soul desire is to be used
An empty vessel longing to be filled by You
My soul desire is to serve You Lord

To do your perfect will
To work each day and build
Your Kingdom, this is my soul desire.

How many times would I sing myself to sleep with this song as a prayer? The worst lies are those we try to convince ourselves of. People would tell me how courageous I was for smiling in the face of what life or God depending on their beliefs had given me: "Whatever doesn't kill you makes you stronger." I was a stronger person and would be better for this experience. I learned to smile and thank people based on the good intentions behind the comments. At times during the day, I was almost proud of myself, but at night, any false pretense came crashing down like a house of cards.

Living every day is not a Nike or Gatorade commercial as inspiring as they are. I imagined the Just Do It commercial with the music and my getting up and putting on my pants in the morning. Somehow, the courage and strength required to pull on sweatpants fell more into the category of comedy rather than inspiration; I was proud of myself for my achievement, but it was far from enough to be something to live for.

Most mornings, I woke up, looked at the time, sighed, and thought, *Only twelve … fourteen … hours until it's time to go to bed.* Worse was waking up from a dream and swinging my legs up only to remember just in time that I didn't have legs. In milliseconds, I experienced loss again. Upon waking, reality crashed down and sucked all the air out of me.

There is a difference between existing and living. Everyone needs a purpose, a reason to live, hopes. Years later, Rick Warren wrote *The Purpose Driven Life*, and based on the book's popularity, I stand today vindicated in the place I found myself in all those years ago. To truly live and not simply exist requires purpose. I am grateful for the silence that filled those days. I had a Walkman that required batteries. We did not have Atari or cable TV. I had to share space with my family, so my boombox was not accessible, and I had time to think and read and think and process.

By the end of the holidays when it was time to return to the hospital, I knew that the only way I could continue living is if I trusted God that all these things were according to His purpose and that I had to hold on to that tightly.

CHAPTER 7

Finding Truth in Despair

I was actually looking forward to going back to the hospital, a place where I felt independent and had a modicum of privacy. Best of all, I would be able to use a toilet, a for-real porcelain throne that flushed.

In the second week of January 1988, I returned to Madison University Hospital. Monday through Friday would be intense therapy, but I would spend weekends at home. I had to be back by ten every Sunday night. I got back much sooner because my parents accompanied me on that first trip though I drove my car and would be driving independently from then on, and of course they had to make the three-hour drive back home.

One of my first visits was to the burn unit to see the nurses there. Everyone there was a little more subdued than normal. I found out that a young man in his early twenties was in a curtained room; his life was held in the balance because of meningococcal meningitis. His amputations were more severe; he had lost his legs below the knee and an arm above the elbow, and his hand lost all of its fingers except half a thumb. Unlike me, the decision had been made to keep him in an induced coma until he had healed more and stabilized. He also had Hodgkin's lymphoma, which was complicating his recovery.

Then the quiet question came: Would I mind talking to his

family in the waiting room? Of course I would talk to them; it was the right thing to do, but anxiety welled up in my stomach all the same. My emotions were often all I could handle, and I knew that I was rolling out into a hurricane of emotions. Even so, I had calm in my heart that I didn't recognize for what it was. I did have joy from the Holy Spirit that enabled me to have an easy smile and compassion for others.

The nurse led me out the door normally used only by doctors and nurses to the ICU waiting room. One group out there looked questionably at the nurse and me as we approached. The nurse introduced us and explained our connection and why I was there. There were tears, there was show and tell, there were questions, and finally there were hugs and thank-yous. I told them where my room was if they had more questions or wanted to talk; I said I would come to see how J was doing. I think they had a little more hope when I rolled away. I had more gratitude for my rat claw, and I was grateful to have been able to help ease in some small way their disturbed hearts and minds.

The next morning, I met with my team of rehab doctors, interns, residents, therapists, and my prosthetist. They were excited about my progress and were optimistic about my future ability to walk. I almost believed them. I had daydreamed of the prosthetics. I was told that I would be a calorie-burning machine using my prosthetics, and I saw myself as fit and beautiful! At that point, I had to bring myself back to reality before I became a TV show in my mind.

Well, when I rolled into the PT room and saw my new legs with size eight Reeboks on them, I was less than enthusiastic. My sarcastic mind had already taken me back to the dark ages, and what lay before me were the instruments of torture to which I would be subjected. I tried to regroup and prayed that I could see these as my ticket to independence. It was January in Wisconsin, and wheelchairs and snow are not a good combination, so perhaps my forays outdoors could provide further motivation.

The prosthetics did not look like anything I had seen on TV or in magazines; they looked more like leg braces. I had been told to bring shorts. Sweatpants were my go-to fashion option at that time. Honestly, wearing shorts was only slightly more revealing. I had no skin showing between the Jobst compression garments and the Ace bandages. I quickly realized that I would never be able to wear those prosthetics with anything but shorts. They were a hybrid of leg braces and weight- bearing devices for both a below-knee amputee (on the bony structures of the knee) and an above-knee amputee (one's seat bone, ischial tuberosity). I less than enthusiastically unwrapped my stumps and rerolled my Ace bandages. I was handed a cotton stump sock that looked three feet long. It went from the end of my stump up to my behind. Then I was given a leather sock of sorts called an insert that fit over the sock up to my knee. I threaded my stump through the hard, weight-bearing part that would fit around my thigh between the metal braces and then into the hard socket area into which I slid my stump … very carefully. Repeat with the left side. I hooked myself up to a belt around my waist and was told to stand up between the parallel bars, where my wheelchair was parked. I stood. It was the first time in six months that I was standing.

I was holding on to the bars for dear life not for balance but because I didn't want to put my full weight on those legs. I had imagined that I would be able to just slip these legs on and off like boots, but reality bit me. Some nerves, muscles, blood vessels, and in my case some skin had been relocated to new positions and thus had new functions. It was uncomfortable to say the least, but I was smiling.

The parallel bars were in the center of the PT room, so I had an audience of fellow patients who whooped and whistled though most of them would never stand again. One does not whine in that situation. Not even a little.

I let my full weight down on the legs and took my first steps. When I left the security of the parallel bars, I wasn't allowed to use a walker so that I would stand up straight and almost entirely depend on my legs to walk. I had two canes to assist with balance. On my next session, I did a whole lap around the rehabilitation area with my therapist holding on to my gait belt and me tightly gripping two canes. I was thrilled. More than once I pinched the tender skin on my inner thigh between the hard material. I wasn't expecting that, and it took me by surprise; I let out a screamy-squeally kind of sound, which caught my therapist off guard the first time it happened. All in all, though, success!

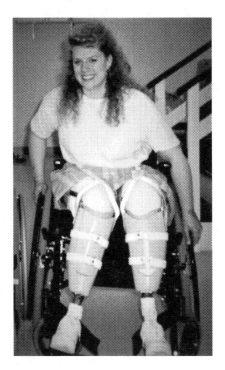

Sitting in the wheelchair wearing prosthetics in the physical therapy room

I sat down in my wheelchair, and we were taking everything off when we saw blood, which everyone had been concerned would happen. It was why my prosthetics had such a strange design. My patella tendon had been exposed under my right knee for months;

I faced the constant threat of making a below-knee amputation an above-knee one.

The graft/scar tissue that had allowed it to heal had adhered to the tendon. Our skin is a magnificent design as a covering, a protective and elastic organ. An amputee is in dire need of that elasticity at weight-bearing points to be able to take the slippage, the movement of the stump in the socket. Just like with a shoe, it should feel as if the foot and shoe are one. The goal is a snug fit; if it is too loose or too tight, the skin will suffer. Even with a perfect fit, some movement in a socket or shoe is inevitable. My scarred skin had no elasticity, so it had simply been torn. I did not feel it as the nerves that would have sent such signals were no longer there; however, when my brain received the signal from my eyes, it decided it must hurt and began sending out the signals of pain. I know it sounds weird, but my nonexistent toes were cold every time I was in the car with snow everywhere also. This is another facet of phantom pains as the brain slowly comes to grips with its loss and compensates for it. With the appearance of blood, the latex gloves and protective gear came out as the doctors were called in to assess the damage.

My prosthetist had done all he could to distribute the weight at different points to relieve the pressure, but they thought a leather pad in that area might be useful. I was assured that this was the beginning of the process. I would need to heal and then try again. I looked at my new wound on top of the old wound that had taken so long to heal and felt my optimism leaving me like a leak in a tire.

I had become quite good at reading body language, eyes, and breathing. The next day when my prosthetist came to pick up my right prosthesis, he wanted to take a look at the wound. His words were hopeful, but his exhale was a little too strong when he saw the damage. The double pat he gave me on my quads as he took his leave confirmed my suspicions. This was not a minor setback.

Then the weekend would arrive. Time to go home. Every weekend, I was helped to my car in the hospital parking lot with my bag of dirty clothes and toiletries. I would purposely drink next to nothing on Fridays so I would have to stop only once on the way home. I enjoyed driving and the solitude during those trips, but once I got home, I was stuck, dependent, a burden to everyone especially because of the dreaded toilet bucket. I was tethered to my wheelchair that wouldn't take me anywhere but around the living room.

I tried to get home in time on Fridays to see my brother's basketball games. I went to church on Sundays and ate lunch before driving back to Madison; I tried to get there early in the evening. It might take me a couple of trips to get stuff up to my room, but I could do it because I wasn't in a rush. That's what I liked most about the hospital; I could do what I needed to do independently compared to being at home.

Otherwise, all those months were a blur of laughter and tears. I have so many memories of things I was a part of or incidents I witnessed, anecdotes that form a general memory. I learned which nurses liked which soap operas and would change the channel accordingly so I would get lunch faster depending on which nurse was on duty. If I had their favorite soaps on, they would check in on me more frequently. I also knew the storyline for every soap opera on the major networks at that time so that I could have a conversation with any nurse about what was happening in his or her favorite soap.

I fondly remember many of my fellow patients. For the most part, the people were what made the hospital comfortable. There were uncomfortable things too like a brain injury patient who had damaged something so that he had to hold his eyelids open. Of course, his brain was damaged as well so that there was no judgment involved—his emotions and instincts took over. If we saw him in the hallway, we would give him a wide berth because he was known to lash out or drop his pants and pee right there in the hall. He couldn't speak clearly, but some words were unmistakable. They were situations that I had never known existed before. We would laugh nervously at these things, but we also had respect because it was a constant reminder of the myriad ways people can be broken.

I became more grateful that my disability had been caused by a bacterium, not another person or my poor judgment. We observed the effects on an entire family whose members had been injured in an accident in which alcohol had been a major factor; that was the case for about half the patients in rehabilitation, and it was the impairment of one of the parents that had caused their accident. Living with that was in many ways harder than the physical disability, which seemed impossible. Group therapy gave me tremendous insight into how different people thought about, responded to, or said in the face of tragedy.

We had weekly outings for movies, trips to the mall, wheelchair dancing, and swimming. We'd get locked down like cargo in a van equipped for wheelchairs. Most of us loved swimming, but we were all so messed up and broken that we laughed so hard at ourselves in and out of the water; we could share certain things that way and laugh; I doubt anyone else could understand, but it brought us together. Those of us who were independent in our wheelchairs figured out how to push our friends who weren't. Then there were incidents with other patients and especially the brain injuries who were mobile and quite honestly scared us sometimes, but later, we would laugh and talk about how our sitcom in the hospital would play out.

Friendship, awkwardness, loss, and most tragically death. We were on the rehab floor, but we shared an elevator with pediatrics, and some of the pediatric patients would go on outings to the movies and such with us until they couldn't. Those laughing boys who had run their remote-control car around my wheelchair when I first got to rehab back in October became my opponents in epic battles of Connect Four, Parcheesi, and other games in the rehab area. While I got stronger, they got weaker until they couldn't go out anymore with us to, say, movies. Then they couldn't have visitors anymore. Leukemia took them in the same month. I avoided that elevator after that.

We would hear about friends who had been discharged, caught pneumonia, and died of complications. Then we were silent because our friend next to us in the halo had the injury in her spinal cord at the same level and our unspoken thought was that something like that could take her too. I tried to put my pain into perspective. Back in the PT gym, my prosthetics were waiting. I would wear them just for a time, and after doing that for a week, I would try standing between the parallel bars. Finally, I would walk the hallway that formed a block around the rehab area and be successful for a time, and then the skin would break. Again. The process would begin anew with testing different skin protocols to see if there would be any improvement. On one occasion, I even got to race sort of with a fellow meningococcal survivor from the burn unit in our prosthetics. He was quiet and reserved, but that day, even he was smiling. Though I had had a six-month head start on him, he was walking much better and more consistently than I was. He needed help to get all his prosthetics on, but then he did great. I however was sitting in my wheelchair waiting for my skin to heal most of the time. It was a roller-coaster of emotions, of progress and setbacks between home and the hospital. In the end though, it was a loop.

In April, I learned that I would need surgery for a bone spur on my other stump. I couldn't hold it together. So many of the people I had met had already gone home, and I hadn't improved at all and was going to have yet another surgery. How many times had we tried a new solution that would help my skin tolerate the prosthetics that hadn't worked? Hadn't I told them to take care of both sides at once when they removed the first bone spur? Did these doctors really know what they were doing? They had this fancy repertoire of technical medical words that they used repeatedly. All the months of my hoping to walk again had been deferred again. Disappointment, anger, and frustration piled on me and leaked out right there as my tears flowed onto the PT mat.

Dr. H said little as he examined me. He spent maybe all of ten seconds palpating the end of my stump where the bone spur was. His work was in those skin grafts, and he was pinching and pulling with undivided attention. My largest graft was on my behind. The outline of the gaping crater was visible even through thick sweatpants. There I was lying prone while Dr. H was spending a long time with this one. Finally, he started saying something while I was in a most awkward position without sweatpants. I understood about 75 percent of what he said, but I don't think he was really talking to me anyway.

There was a silver lining to my cloud of gloom. He was going to close that crater up with sutures something ... something. I would recover in the burn unit as they needed to order this or that. After Dr. H slipped out, the burn nurses translated for him; he would use different kinds of thicker sutures to close the crater as I called it, and to recover, I would move to the burn unit and use a special, nonpressure air bed filled with air and blowing sand. The powerful blower could be turned off in case the patient coded; the sand would make a solid surface upon which a patient could be revived or in my case more easily transfer or be transferred out of the bed. They knew how badly I had reacted to the anesthesia and were prepared for that, but the bad news was that this bed did not travel, so the radiation treatments meant a few transfers.

Everything happened as it had during my last surgery except that I was in the burn unit. I healed there from the bone spur and several revisions of my soft tissue on my elbow, stump, and posterior. Stitches like electrical wire were finally removed from there, and I returned to the rehab floor.

My rehab team met again shortly afterward. The decision was made that no more progress could be achieved with in-patient care, so on April 23, I was discharged. I was to return two days a week for therapy. It was a bittersweet moment.

Home just didn't feel like home should—comfortable. I think I simply didn't feel comfortable in my own body and therefore didn't feel this was a familiar place where I could do the things I used to do and spend time in the places I used to spend time. I had always hoped that coming home would mean continuing with the life I used to lead just with a few modifications, but that was not the case.

Construction had nearly been completed on the wheelchair-accessible bedroom and bathroom. In my restlessness, I even scooted up the stairs to my bedroom one bum hop at a time. It was eerie looking at the room I had left so many months before. I rummaged through what I could reach sitting on the floor. So many memories and hopes from a life that had ended.

That might sound dramatic, but embracing a new normal as many therapists say requires grieving and accepting the loss of the old normal, but that was not an easy or automatic decision of the will in a moment; it was a gradual realization that this was not just a rough patch to get through. How many times had I found myself saying, "When I get better ..." There I was out of the hospital except for two days a week and was not better in the way I had been thinking about better, but I was better. *Better Off Dead* was the name of a 1985 high school romance comedy movie and what I used to mutter to myself whenever I caught myself thinking these thoughts, which was a little more often than I care to admit.

Being out of the hospital always brought the reality of my situation into sharp focus. Willpower can make you stronger, and determination can keep you going, but as I had painfully learned over the past four months since January was that neither could stop my skin from breaking down. If pain is gain, I should have gained a whole lot more than I had.

That afternoon as I sifted through the past and present, I realized that even if my life had gone on normally or as I had planned, marriage and living in a different country, I would be facing huge goodbyes and equally huge changes. The Lord whispered as He so often does if I would just listen, "Have you not gained anything through your pain?" Gently, slowly, the memories came to me as I held things in my hands that represented who I had been and compared that to how I thought about people, issues, and things in my new present. I realized I had been changing, growing, and even becoming stronger than I had been. I was much more honest and aware than I had ever been and much more than I would have been if I had continued normally in my life. This was a landmark moment of acceptance, which is not giving up; it's a surrender to God but not to circumstances. Acceptance is a start, not an end, a level, strong foundation that can be built upon.

As I carefully scooted back downstairs, I said my goodbyes to the Pam I had been and again decided to face the reality of now, not what could be, but just today. I began to see tomorrow from a wheelchair. "But one thing I do: forgetting what is behind and straining toward what is ahead"; that verse would pop into my head. Having been a PK for most of my life, I had memorized some and become familiar with most of the Bible. The words seemed to take on life for me as I sat and had no real distractions. Years ago, someone had placed a large picture of Jesus on the narrow wall at the bottom of the stairs. I took a break from my scooting, and "looking unto Jesus the pioneer and perfecter of faith" popped into my head. I remembered those two verses well enough but not where they were in the Bible. There I was in the late eighties with no Google, so I was forced to use something that is probably considered archaic today, a Bible concordance, to find them; I just knew there was more to them, and I found them, the first one in Philippians.

Not that I have already obtained all this, or have already arrived at my goal, but I press on to take hold of that for which Christ Jesus took hold of me. Brothers and sisters, I do not consider myself yet to have taken hold of it. But one thing I do: Forgetting what is behind and straining toward what is ahead, I press on toward the goal to win the prize for which God has called me heavenward in Christ Jesus.

All of us, then, who are mature should take such a view of things. And if on some point you think differently, that too God will make clear to you. Only let us live up to what we have already attained.

Join together in following my example, brothers and sisters, and just as you have us as a model, keep your eyes on those who live as we do. For, as I have often told you before and now tell you again even with tears, many live as enemies of the cross of Christ. Their destiny is destruction, their god is their stomach, and their glory is in their shame. Their mind is set on earthly things. But our citizenship is in heaven. And we eagerly await a Savior from there, the Lord Jesus Christ, who, by the power that enables him to bring everything under his control, will transform our lowly bodies so that they will be like his glorious body. (Philippians 3:12–21 NIV)

These were verses I had read and even studied numerous times in my life, but all of a sudden they just jumped to life for me and I understood them clearly. For perhaps the first time, I heard Paul speaking these words, God's words, not in the tone of a self-righteous, angry deacon preaching at me but in a sincere, passionate, almost pleading tone as the apostle Paul entreated me to understand along with him. I imagined him sitting on the floor with me as I read the words again. This is what I understood Paul saying so clearly in my paraphrase of Philippians 3:12–21.

Pam, I haven't earned my own salvation, and I'm not perfect, but I do as much as I possibly can to become so because Jesus Christ paid the price for me. He has made me His own just like you. Pam, I don't think I'm worthy or perfect, but this is what I do. I forget what lies behind, you know, the mistakes, the betrayal, the sins, the guilt, the fear, the pain … and I keep pushing forward. I know it's not easy to move forward; sometimes, we have to put all our weight behind it. Pam, push forward to what lies ahead. Push toward the goal, the prize that is God's upward and sometimes difficult call that we have received in Jesus Christ. Let those of us who are mature think like this, but if you don't right now, God will reveal that to you too. But Pam, hold on to what you do know.

Pam, agree with us and follow the example of those who have followed God's call in their lives despite anything that happened to them here on earth. There are so many people who do not believe, people whose decisions make them walk as enemies of the cross of Christ. Pam, cry for them! The end of their life will be destruction; they are ruled by their physical bodies and desires; too often, what they are so proud of is meaningless and before God shameful because it is sinful and selfish and because they had nothing to do with the gift God gave them to begin with, but they can't see that because their minds are fixed on the here and now.

But Pam, we are citizens of heaven! [In my mind's eye, Paul gestures a lot. Here, he goes from pointing to the ground to pointing up to heaven as he raises his head and smiles.] From heaven, we wait for our Savior, the Lord Jesus Christ! He will transform our lowly bodies to be like His glorious body by the power and authority He has over all things. Pam, you belong to Him! We are living now for that day!

I found the second verse in Hebrews 12. Hebrews 11 mentions the hall of famers in terms of faith in God and the obstacles they overcame. Chapter 12 flows out as a continuation of it.

> Therefore, since we are surrounded by such a great cloud of witnesses, let us throw off everything that hinders and the sin that so easily entangles. And let us run with perseverance the race marked out for us, fixing our eyes on Jesus, the pioneer and perfecter of faith. For the joy set before him he endured the cross, scorning its shame, and sat down at the right hand of the throne of God. (Hebrews 12:1–2 NIV)

The writer of Hebrews was encouraging us to look at the examples of those witnesses of faith and to endure and overcome. If that wasn't enough reason, we can look at Jesus Himself. He endured the cross and despised the shame for the joy that was set before Him. That future was set before me.

Those two verses reminded me of something I had been convinced of earlier—that something greater is waiting for those who call Jesus Christ Lord. I decided not for the first and certainly not for the last time to get up off the floor and to run or at least roll with endurance; the race set before me was not going to be easy.

I started by helping out with kids again. Certain things make me laugh, especially little kids. This three-year-old would run up to my wheelchair every Sunday to tell me, "You ain't got no feets." The look on his face bore no malice; he was simply letting me know that in case I hadn't noticed.

One time, I had gone to the store and was waiting to check out. I felt a tug on my jeans that made me lean forward and look down. A boy who had lain on his back under my wheelchair had grabbed the hem of one pantleg with both little hands and was looking intently to discover where I had put my feet I guessed. His eyes met mine about the same time his mom realized where he was and what he was up to. I was smiling, but she was mortified and dragged him out of the store before I could say anything. One little girl honestly told me that my hands were "*ree*ally" ugly, but after a pause, she added, "but God loves you, and so do I." She gave me a hug, and from then on, all our interactions were as normal as could be. A lot of younger kids wanted to touch the nubs on my hands, and after that, they were satisfied. I never knew what would come out of a child's mouth, but I learned that once a child had satisfied his or her curiosity, everything would be OK.

Day followed day. Sunday was church. Midweek was the three-hour drive to the hospital. My PT therapist let me spend the night at her place to do both my days at the hospital. At least those days broke up the monotony.

The bedroom and bathroom addition at the parsonage was wonderful for me, and it served another purpose; it had a door that led to a patio outside that connected to the side door of the church. That way, church members who had difficulty navigating stairs could use the addition's bathroom instead of the bathrooms in the church basement. The door opened into my room, and the bathroom could be accessed from there. I had to make sure my bedroom and bathroom were completely picked up and things put away on Sunday mornings and evenings and Wednesday nights. It's not as if I had any secrets or valuables that I needed to hide, but I had long since learned that it takes only a little thing to get people speculating on the doings of the preacher's daughter, and I was a person of great suspect given that I had so recently been engaged to a foreigner and had planned to live in Spain. I had heard the hushed, wild theories of some—that I had gotten sick because Antonio had brought over some foreign disease with him or even that this is what happens to people who graduate early from high school instead of respecting established times and seasons.

In another way, the addition served as a very real object lesson for me that the Lord wanted me to understand. As the song goes, "This world is not my home, I'm just a-passing through."[6] That house did not belong to us, and the addition was mine only in the sense that I had it for a time to use. For the short time that room was mine, I had lots of time to think things through. Quite a few people even encouraged me to write, but what they couldn't know was that my hurt was deeper than my physical disability, that the Lord wasn't going to restore me to who I had been. He was going to continue debriding my heart, mind, and soul. His healing was going to go deeper than flesh and blood.

Jesus has a habit of reordering lives. He doesn't quietly enter someone's life and take a seat in the corner. He tends to flip over the tables, force abrupt career changes, spill things, redistribute wealth, cause stumbling, and perform miracles on His terms. I've also experienced no small amount of weeping and shouting in the process. Jesus causes major changes that sometimes we call miracles. I didn't do Jesus a favor by inviting Him into my heart. He has no need of me; I had every need of Him, and to invite Him into my life required radical reconstruction. C. S. Lewis wrote,

> Imagine yourself as a living house. God comes in to rebuild that house. At first, perhaps, you can understand what He is doing. He is getting the drains right and stopping the leaks in the roof and so on; you knew that those jobs needed doing and so you are not surprised. But presently He starts knocking the house about in a way that hurts abominably and does not seem to make any sense. What on earth is He up to? The explanation is that He is building quite a different house from the one you thought of - throwing out a new wing here, putting on an extra floor there, running up towers, making courtyards. You thought you were being made into a decent little cottage: but He is building a palace. He intends to come and live in it Himself.[7]

The King of Kings and Lord of Lords does not live in places made by human hands but in those He has constructed. At age nineteen, I could see how God had worked through my experiences and decisions up until that time to pour a solid foundation. He had been preparing me to be able to withstand this trial. The walls I had built had been torn down, and all my belongings had been destroyed. I was feeling totally exposed and vulnerable; God allowed me to be poked and prodded in all those places I tried so desperately to keep hidden and protected. My healing and transformation had only just started, and I would never recover from that.

When I was young, I used to think that the older I became, the more I would be prepared and have it all together in a kind of arrival of sorts, but that was not the case either. My visits to the small apartment of Miss Ruth, who was in her late eighties at that time, demonstrated her total dependence on God, not her mastery of the Christian life. It was not so much about being X and doing Y but simply trusting and surrendering. I remembered some people on the radio and in conversations in Christian circles talking about the gift of singleness. At the time, I was a teenager who thought I would never fall in love or ever marry, so I asked her if she thought she had the gift of singleness. I remember her gentle reply as she smiled ever so slightly, "Oh no! I gave God every chance for me to find a husband, but He never saw fit to do that, so I just learned to live with it."

Her answers always surprised me. She was always so patient with my lack of dedication to studying the gospel with her, but she invited me over all the same and patiently answered my questions about her life in China and Malaysia. I was taken aback with all the adventures, dangers, and frustrations she had faced. She was using a walker, but her feet had walked hundreds of miles across mainland China. She had served there after having accepted to God's call to the mission field as a teenager.

I listened to her stories with great enthusiasm and amazement at what this frail, old woman had lived through. The one thing I knew for sure about Miss Ruth was that she was a real Christian; she loved Jesus, and she loved to talk about Him. She had lived an amazingly full life and continued to serve God even when her body was failing and she was living alone in a tiny apartment.

I realized just how real and relevant God was to her. He was not someone with the long beard somewhere up in heaven, a distant, fictional character of her imagination or a god that she just brought out on Sundays at church. To her, He was the God who loved her and cared for her in any situation; she had seen Him intervene many times in her life and in the lives of people around her. God was her constant companion, but He was also the God of heaven, and Jesus was the one to whom she owed everything. Even then, as a teenager, that gave me pause. Her prayers were always so different from other people's because I really felt she was talking to God, not to me or for my benefit and never to impress others. I wondered about some of the things she prayed for. One of my treasured possessions is a card she gave me before I left on my summer mission trip before high school. She wrote a quotation from John 10:4 (KJV) on how Jesus is our good Shepherd. The phrase that stood out the most and I would reflect on with tears more than once was simply, "He goes before."

Miss Ruth could have had no idea how much I would need to believe that just a few years later. On that summer mission trip, I would come to memorize a verse that would lead me to this chapter of the Bible that would help me immensely and become an ingrained part of my testimony for the rest of my life. In 2 Corinthians 4:5 (NIV), we read, "For we preach not ourselves, but Christ Jesus as Lord, and ourselves your servants for Christ's sake." We had to memorize this verse mainly to help us remember that whatever activity we were involved in whether singing, playing with kids, being a tourist, or taking on kitchen duty was not about us but about serving God.

Living together in close quarters in tents or on floors, sleeping in sleeping bag, riding the same bus, and working long hours for eight weeks led to our getting on each other's nerves. This verse was the attitude checker for that summer. As with most things in God's time, at the right moment, this verse would pop into my mind in those situations where I was needing an attitude check.

Since coming home in April, the muddy slush was turning into puddles. The days were longer and brighter. Spring finally arrived in the middle of Wisconsin in May. This was in sharp contrast to the inner turmoil that continued to plague me. Every day was a challenge; it required an adjustment of my mind to the situation of my body. The pain of the burn unit and then the discomfort of the Jobst garments had been constant reminders of my physical situation. But in May, I was allowed to remove the Jobsts forever. I was supposed to continue using Ace bandages to wrap my stumps, but I got lazy at night and just wanted to sleep in my own skin as it were.

There was one problem with that, however; my phantom pain got a lot worse. I would wake up at night with a horrible Charlie horse in my calf screaming for attention. I would sit up and put a hand to the place where I was supposedly having so much pain and land it solidly on my mattress. As soon as I could wake up enough to realize what was happening, I would jam my stump into my pillow as hard as I could to tell my nerves that that was their end, not where the pain signals were supposedly coming from. The bandage had applied pressure on the new nerve endings in the amputated limbs, but the lack of pressure allowed the nerves to channel signals like a severed electrical wire. My brain and nerves went on trying to reconcile what was and what is. I had experienced a previous landmark moment of emotional acceptance, but these incidences and others had a way of throwing me off balance. It was exhausting. Many days at home, I would just wake up, look to the ceiling, and wonder how I was ever going to get through the day and hope I would be back in bed soon.

Some nights, my ears filled with tears though I could quickly clean them out and blow my nose. Still, the emotional pain remained, so I would talk to God about how I was feeling in the situation He had left me in. Even so, once I was up and dressed, there was strength to do what needed doing and to interact with people that day.

I would drive to Madison dutifully and enjoy concerts in the park, going out to eat, and all things wheelchair accessible. Then I would return home to Greenwood and find myself in a world not nearly as wheelchair friendly. By that time, I was taking seriously the questions my vocational counselor had posed to me; she wanted me to consider going to the University of Madison because the buses were handicap accessible and the university was fully accessible while my Christian college was not. I agreed with her that it would be very difficult for me to manage classes in almost any of the buildings that were on campus then. Chapel was mandatory, but there was no elevator down to the chapel. I'd not be able to attend many student events and activities, which concerned my vocational counselor for my emotional health.

I had easily decided what my career would be. I had a minor in Spanish and was just six credits away from having it as my major. I had nearly finished an English major, but I still needed a few courses. I had thought about what I could do and live with and had decided on secondary education in English and Spanish. I submitted my transcript to Madison University and learned that many of my classes would not transfer.

Ironically, I had chosen to enter a career in education. Having never been a fan of school, I had just wanted to finish as soon as possible. My plan had been to finish my English major in three years, graduate, go to Spain, and get married. Now with an education component to add on to my Spanish and English degrees, which included a semester of student teaching, I was looking at two more years minimum before I would graduate.

Madison is a beautiful city with four beautiful lakes, and a big part of me really wanted to just pick up and go to the university there for a fresh start, a place where I could be comfortable in a wheelchair and be among a large wheelchair population, but I had a feeling I could not shake that going to Madison was not what I was supposed to do. So I kept putting off coming up with a definitive answer.

In theory, I was supposed to have graduated in the spring of 1989. I decided I needed to go back to attend the graduation ceremony and face what should have been my graduation. I wanted to meet these difficult moments head-on. Besides, I had been invited by Sara, my friend and roommate who had gone to Spain with me.

Back at the college, everything was again surreal, but I tried to put on a good face and blend in with the crowd as I had done before being legless in a wheelchair, but now go anywhere without being noticed for good and bad reasons, a constant reminder that I was not the person I had been. I was totally dependent on others to get where I wanted to go. I had to repeatedly explain how my footrests were removed and put back on and how the wheelchair folded. I have never been small or even medium, and it terrified and embarrassed me every time someone had to lift my wheelchair with me in it when we encountered stairs. Inevitably, someone would hold on to the wheels instead of the frame. The wheels would spin even though they had been locked because of the pressure; the person would lose grip on those spinning wheels and the frame would rotate, which in turn would cause me to slip out of the chair. Everyone would end up feeling embarrassed. It was emotionally exhausting.

Nonetheless, stairs were manageable, but the same was not true of doorways that were too narrow for the wheelchair; they were impassable until I started doing something which was incredibly frowned upon by my doctors and therapists—crawling around on my knees. Most bathrooms were not ADA compliant in the late eighties, so crawling was the only way I could make an inaccessible bathroom accessible for me. It is a very humbling experience to be on one's hands and knees on the bathroom floor. How fitting then that bathrooms were where I was alone and could let tears leak out and plead with God to please release me from this life. I would reach my hands up to the sink like a three-year-old with about the same motor skills due to my missing fingers, and water would drip off my elbows. I would then put on my bike gloves and brace myself to face the world again.

Graduation day arrived. I was sitting next to Sara's fiancé, Antonio's friend. The darkness in me bubbled up to a boiling point as uninvited sarcastic questions and comments circled in my head faster and louder. I could barely breathe. To leave in the middle of the speeches would draw too much attention to myself, so I was trapped. I just wanted to literally die right there. I prayed I would, but I knew it was far more likely that I'd just lose consciousness and make more of a spectacle of myself. I fixed my eyes on a point and tried breathing through my nose as my throat painfully constricted and floating lights danced across my field of vision. *Oh God! Dear Lord, help me! I can't do this! I can't!* Mercifully, music started, and everyone stood and began to sing the hymn that came next in the program.

1. Great is thy faithfulness, O God my father,
   there is no shadow of turning with thee;
   thou changest not, thy compassions, they fail not
   as thou hast been thou forever wilt be.

   Chorus:
   Great is thy faithfulness! great is thy faithfulness!
   Morning by morning new mercies I see;
   all I have needed thy hand hath provided.
   Great is thy faithfulness Lord unto me!

2. Summer and winter, and springtime and harvest,
   sun, moon and stars in their courses above,
   join with all nature in manifold witness
   to thy great faithfulness, mercy and love.

3. Pardon for sin and a peace that endureth,
   thine own dear presence to cheer and to guide;
   strength for today and bright hope for tomorrow,
   blessings all mine, with ten thousand beside![8]

While the audience stood to sing, I was safely guarded in my sitting position with my head bowed over the program and my hair shielding my face as my tears poured out. I whispered the chorus as the voices around me belted out the familiar hymn. I wasn't hearing it as the chorus of praise I knew. That time, the hymn sounded like a promise. My thoughts miraculously transformed to focus on the many things I had to be thankful for, all the times God had seen me through and would see me through. I cannot explain it, but the darkness in me became light. I could breathe again. The promise came again, "Pam, wherever I ask you to go; I go before."

From that time on, I confidently and faithfully trusted in the Lord. I wish I could write that. I know it's a lot of the reason I hadn't written sooner. I kept waiting to be able to say that, but three decades have passed since that spring; I'm still waiting to be able to say that 100 percent each moment. So many people have commented on my faith and strength, but I know myself better. All I am able to say truthfully is that God is faithful and that His mercy and grace have carried me through each struggle, failure, and pain.

CHAPTER 8

A Season of Seeking

⚜

I n late May, I received an invitation to come to Camp Forest Springs, a Christian camp in Wisconsin, for their summer activities. I was interviewed and asked to be a part of their camp program sharing my testimony of what had happened to me, what God had taught me, and how He had been faithful to me. I was happy to do that. Then I was told that I would be the camp's missionary project that summer; they would take an offering that would assist me with living expenses needed to finish my education. I was uncomfortable with that. It was gently though firmly explained to me that my discomfort stemmed from misplaced pride.

I was familiar with that concept. I fought to be fiercely independent; I took pride in my ability to do things by myself. While self-reliance is in general a positive trait, as with all things, there comes a point when it can be carried needlessly to an extreme.

My brother was the first to confront me with my pride issue. As soon as I became strong enough to travel independently, I became almost militantly opposed to anyone touching my wheelchair. I would make loud proclamations about cutting off the handles on my wheelchair and putting on a bumper sticker that read Ignorance Should Be Painful. The message was loud and clear—I don't want your help! However, I still did and do need help, like the more times than I care to admit that my wheelchair rolled away from me down an incline when I was taking it out of my car or when I would pump gas but not be able to go in and pay because of a tall curb. (That was in the day before we started swiping credit cards at the pump.) Relying on the help of strangers is embarrassing beyond belief; the fact that I needed others' help could be powerfully infuriating as well as motivating.

Those who knew me realized that my drive for self-sufficiency was motivated by pride more than necessity. My family knew I needed to successfully learn to maneuver my wheelchair in everyday situations. I managed just fine at that point; I was just being stubborn.

One day when I was wrestling my wheelchair over some curb or up an incline or something, I caught a glimpse of my brother looking uncomfortable. His shoulders were slumped, and his hands were jammed into his pockets. For the first time, I realized that *my* actions were causing that look of his. He respected my right to independence, but I was making this six-one young man look on helplessly while I struggled. My message of I don't want your help could all too easily slip into I don't want you or I don't need you.

Pride kills relationships, and I didn't want that. I saw the pain my pride of independence was inflicting written all over him. It wasn't as if I didn't have plenty of opportunities to struggle on my own and get stronger and problem solve in that process. I sighed deeply and relinquished control. His energetic personality returned, and we enjoyed some great conversations as he pushed me along when we were together. (That's not to say he didn't scare me to death accidentally and on purpose. To this day, he is a little brother who still likes to provoke his older sister.)

I had an epiphany that day. My desire for independence was alienating me. Helping someone else was wonderful, but receiving help was excruciating. True love works in both directions—giving and receiving. Pride made me see pity when it was simply a desire to connect with me and help. Pride made every action and look all about me and how I felt; that moment with my brother was eye-opening because I observed his actions and feelings instead of only mine; love does that. Allowing someone to help me was difficult, but I learned that it opened a way for that person to have enough of a comfort zone to connect personally with me or simply allowed others opportunities to show kindness; that was in itself a kindness that was evident in their faces and body language.

But I was in the camp director's office before I had learned that lesson. The thought of receiving more money from others' donations grated on me. His daughter went to my college and was dating one of my friends. He knew more about my situation than I cared to admit. I told him that the money could go to real missionaries or nonprofit ministries instead like Joni and Friends (Joni Eareckson Tada, a quadriplegic since 1967) an international Christian ministry that worked with the disabled. I didn't need anyone's money. Ahh, there it was again. I was thinking, *I didn't need anyone!* but that quiet, barely audible but unmistakable voice said, *That's not true.*

The camp director asked me questions about practical matters such as laundry, when I was going back to school, and modifications needed in an apartment or house. The laundromat was not an option for me any longer without asking for help. The financial burdens had been heavy on my family even before I became sick. I had worked two jobs and took out student loans to offset tuition, medical bills, car payments, and traveling costs in addition to the regular cost of living were added up. I bowed my head, slowly nodded, and exhaled a resigned "OK."

I was determined to do a good job. I was also determined not to lie, gloss over matters, or mislead others in any way. I still wrestled and questioned my emotions, myself, and God, but I was intellectually convinced of the many truths in God's Word. I decided to keep the parts I still struggled with between God and me and focus on what I had resolved and could confidently speak. I prayed about what exactly I would say. In my car on the way to camp, I told God I was not at all confident in this messed-up speaker for this camp, but in the same breath, I said I would be grateful to have something good come out of this.

Once most people talked with me, they felt that at least their problems weren't as bad as mine. I had always struggled with negativity and doubt, but it seemed to intensify by a factor of ten after I had agreed to do this. I was still so raw inside. I spent quite a bit of time following up on the verses that popped into my head during the day, but at night, I found the doubts gnawing at my heart with that sarcastic, biting voice incessantly interrogating me until I could barely breathe. I would finally fall asleep again midprayer or midsong.

Here is another song that I hadn't heard since that summer mission trip years earlier, but it just came back.

> I go to the Rock of my salvation
> I go to the Stone that the builders rejected
> Run to the Mountain and the Mountain stands by me
> The earth all around me is sinking sand
> On Christ, the solid Rock, I stand
> When I need a shelter
> When I need a friend
> I go to the Rock[9]

Just to be clear, the Rock a.k.a. Mr. Dwayne Johnson was a high school football player at this time with his days as the Rock still several years in front of him. The song "The Rock" referred to the original Rock, Jesus Christ. In this conflict of day and night, light and darkness, and faith and doubt, I worked on what I would say. I kept following up Bible verses and settled on 2 Corinthians 4. Like so many other lessons God has placed before me, this chapter would keep growing deeper and deeper in its significance for me over the years. In those days, however, I needed rock holds, places I could just hold on to with conviction. I took this responsibility of speaking about God seriously. I would give no room for my doubt. I would say what and why I believed what I believed, but I did not enter the how because the how to when it came to overcoming struggles eluded me.

There would be five weeks of youth camps followed by four weeks of family camp. I attended an orientation week and saw a couple of people from college and met more from other Christian colleges. There were permanent staff on site in addition to those who would stay for the five weeks of youth camp. Most of them were college students many of whom were completing required experiences and credits for their degrees. Only a handful of counselors would remain to lead the breakout sessions for young people during family camp.

The camp was not handicap accessible as was the case with most places in the eighties, so I was anxious about the experience, but I had the peace of knowing that this is where I was supposed to be. While not at all looking forward to being dependent on others to get around, I was excited to be in a beautiful place with people my age who shared my beliefs.

I stayed in a room in the nurses' trailer close to the central part of camp. Nothing about it was handicap accessible, but I didn't care. My role at camp was limited, and I felt welcomed and appreciated. I had long conversations and laughed until I cried. I answered questions as honestly as I could. Sarcastic humor was how I shocked others to deflect from the topics that were too difficult. I did open up a lot to the friends I made there.

An important, memorable, and even sacred moment came one night when we were around a campfire before camp officially opened. We were asked to join hands, but I never wanted to make anyone feel obliged to grab hold of my rat claw. We weren't in an orderly circle, just sort of jumbled about, so I thought I could escape contact. But no, one of my favorite friends, who was on my left side, took my left hand in hers. I fought back tears unsuccessfully. The ugly places, the hurtful places have to be touched by love before deep healing and acceptance can take place. Melissa acted like Jesus; I would later reflect on this as I realized more deeply why Jesus made it a point to touch when He healed.

The camp, an intimate place before the campers arrived, became alive with action and sound. I was kind of a camp fixture. Most people would give me sideways glances and perhaps a hello but not much more. I enjoyed just sitting back and observing and praying. The counselors were actively engaged with their campers, so I just parked my wheelchair out of the way of the activity without giving in to the urge to hide somewhere. Before I spoke, I always prayerfully read Psalm 51 to help me find the words to confess my myriad of failings, sin, and doubt, and then I would read Isaiah 40 to help prepare my heart.

Memory gets filtered through the present, so to accurately represent myself back then, I used a transcript from a taped session from one week at camp. At that time, I was still nineteen; not even a full year had passed since I had contracted the bacterial meningitis that had so altered my life. I still spent two days a week in Madison. I spent over half an hour in the bathroom each time before I spoke. Thankfully, that bathroom was handicap accessible. When I came up front to speak, it took a little while for me to get situated and assessed by my young audience. I spent less than seven minutes talking about the hospital, and I told them about my frustrating experience of opening the door and catching my Bible by the cover. The following is a transcript what I said at the high school camp.

And I got out in November before Thanksgiving and went around, and people asked me to speak in certain places where I went and I spoke. And I thought, "Hey, I've got three weeks of being there [the hospital in Madison] because I'm going to get my legs, I'm gonna walk, I'm gonna be off to school, I'm gonna be with my friends, and everything's gonna be OK." Because God loves me and He's on my side and I've gone through my trials and I've learned all there is to learn.

You know, I went into the hospital on January 30, and one operation and three months later, I came out still not walking. And here I am before you today still not walking the way that I had hoped and dreamed of, and every week, I have to go to Madison. I have to leave you guys Tuesday night to get to the hospital on Wednesday morning and Thursday to go for therapy in Madison.

Folks, you may look at me now and think, "I hope that never happens to me." You're Christians and maybe you're going, "God, I love you, but don't do that to me!" But I want to tell you that I've learned what's really important. That what you see, that what you see in me—I don't have legs and I don't have fingers—is something that's temporary, and something that really doesn't matter, and that's hard to say. Lots of you guys are dealing with stuff, but I'm here to tell you it really doesn't matter. The world has lied to you and told you that those are the most important things.

Girls, let's talk about one example—your looks. Girls, how much time do we spend in the mirror in the morning? Is it proportional to the time you spend reading the Bible and praying? Your looks are all going to go away someday. Guess what? Your grandmas all looked like you at one time. Your skin is going to sag, and you're going to collect cellulite. I'm sorry, but that's just the way life is, and one day, you're gonna die. It's temporary.

Guys, sports. My brother is a basketball player. Our team won the state championship in 1988. He was on the team. Mr. Basketball himself, he goes to every basketball camp he can find, but what does it matter? He's a high school hero, but then he goes to college and finds guys who are better than him. And what does it matter? One day, Michael Jordan is going to turn sixty, and he's not going to slam dunk anymore. It's temporary; it doesn't last.

There's one thing that will last in your life, one thing that will make a difference, one thing you can stand on, and one thing that will never change. The world will tell you every day through your music, on TV, and at school that having a car is important, being beautiful is important, being successful is important, and having money is important, but folks, all those things can disappear in a day.

I became a Christian when I was four. How do you become a Christian? Somebody tell me. Just say it. What do you do? You ask God into your heart. Somebody tell me, what does that mean? Do you know what that means? We say we accept Jesus into our hearts.

When you pray, what what's one of the things you say when you start to pray? Tell me. "Dear God." What's with another term we use, "heavenly Father"? Another term we use, "Lord"? Do we say "Lord Jesus" a lot? What does that term "Lord" mean? Someone you worship? I know that people in England say, "Lord Winston" or whatever, but what is a lord? Is the Lord a ruler? Yes he is.

What does your heart do? It pumps blood. What else? Girls, if a guy doesn't love you, and when a girl doesn't love you, guys, you say they broke your … heart. It's not only the center of what makes you alive; it's at the center of your emotions. Right or wrong? Right. You say you accept Jesus into your heart and Jesus is the Lord, right? When you say you ask the Lord into your heart, what are you saying? That He's the ruler of your heart, the ruler of your life in other words. He controls you, am I right?

Let me tell you a little story. One day, you're out playing, and it's just rained, and there's a big mud puddle. And you're just really bored, and so you start making little things and make like a little horse and you make like a little tree and you say "Hey!" like a Barbie doll or like a little person and you just go, *Phew!* And it's alive! Hey, dude! He's just looking up at you like, "What should I do?" So you say, "Hey, you can do anything you want, but just don't throw rocks, OK? Don't be throwing rocks because you might hurt somebody or break my tree down, and you know I worked for a long time on that tree, so don't be throwing rocks."

And you go away because somebody called your name or something. and so you have to wait. And you come back and the little guy is walking along the edge of the mud puddle and he kicks in some pebbles, *blup, blup, blup.* That's pretty cool! And you come back when he's picking up a bunch of pebbles. So you say, "Hey, what are you doing? That's not what I said you could do." He tells you, "I'm sorry. I won't do it again. I promise." So you go away, and the little dude watches you leave.

As soon as he thinks you're out of sight, he starts looking for the biggest rock he can find. You're watching him as he lifts that huge rock over his head and throws it in the water—*Pfwoop!* He laughs. He thinks it's funny. And you go to him and pick him up and say, "Hey, I thought I told you not to throw rocks." The little guy is standing like this big in your hand [Show about half an inch between your thumb and index finger], and he looks at you and says, "Get out of my face! I'm not gonna do what you want me to do. Just get out of my face! I want to do what I want to do!"

And what would you do? [sound of a single clap] You're right. You know what, folks? God created you. You know what the Bible says—God holds the waters of this. Listen, listen. The Bible says that God holds all the waters of the earth in the palm of His hand. I can barely imagine him holding the lake out here in the palm of His hand; that's a pretty big hand. That means the Atlantic Ocean and the Pacific Ocean in the palm of His hand. That makes you pretty tiny, but you know what? Every time you disobey, every time you reject God, you stand in His hand and you tell Him, "Get out of my face. I'm going to do what I want to do and don't you ever tell me what to do." He could have smushed you. He could've destroyed you right then and there, and He still has that power, but instead, He sent His Son to die for you.

Because I'm a Christian, I have a place to stand even when I don't have any legs to stand on because Jesus Christ is the basis of my life. I know a seven- and a ten-year-old who died last month of leukemia. Life is temporary. I have a friend on a team we played to get to state. He was a six-five basketball, football, and baseball player who had a college scholarship. On graduation night, he went out drinking. Not a lot, just one or two drinks, but enough that he lost control of his car and rolled it. He's a quadriplegic now. He can't move anything but his head. His life was destroyed in thirty seconds. He told me the story of what had happened to him and said, "I don't have anything to live for." He had no place to stand.

I know a young woman, a fitness nut. She's about five-two, and she has the most perfect body you've ever seen. She ran twenty miles a day for the fun of it! She went on a motorcycle with her drunk boyfriend and ended up in a ditch. She's paralyzed from the neck down. Her life has been destroyed, and she has nothing to live for because her life isn't grounded on Jesus Christ. Something to think about because when it comes right down to it, it's your choice. God is giving you a choice to accept or reject Him. He died for you. You can accept Him, or you can reject Him.

Can you think of anything that will last in this world? If you have a nice car or the most beautiful girlfriend or the most gorgeous boyfriend, will that last? Does it matter? You know, they can go through a windshield and smash up their faces. Money? How many people have gone bankrupt? How quickly is your money spent? It's temporary. Think of anything. Your friends. Friends can be fickle. I have some high school friends who can't even look at me anymore. That's hard to take. But they aren't forever.

I encourage you to think of anything that's forever, anything that will always matter. I tell you that there's no reason to live unless you have your life in Jesus Christ. There's nothing other than that that will ever matter.

One day, I'm gonna stand before God. I'm going to dance at His feet. I'll be whole, and I'll be happy. You guys know the feeling of being at a basketball game against a rival school and it's like you guys are tied and your team pulled it off in overtime. You know the feeling, don't you? You get so excited! You know what I'm talking about. I want to cry and jump up and down when I watch my brother play and win. Heaven is so much more than that. It will make my game look like nothing. Are you gonna be there? What's important?

I want to read you a verse that talks about how things can be hard here. Some pressures you face are real—pressures to wear nice clothes, be a perfect athlete, and so on. And it is hard. In 2 Corinthians 4:16–18 (NIV), we read, "Therefore we do not lose heart though outwardly we are wasting away yet inwardly we are being renewed day by day for light and momentary troubles." The Bible says that what happens to us is light and that momentary troubles "are achieving for us an eternal glory that far outweighs them all," meaning that anything you've ever gone through that was hard won't even compare to what you will see in heaven. "So we fix our eyes not on what is seen but on what is unseen. For what is seen is temporary, but what is unseen is eternal."

Folks, the only thing that will ever matter is what we do with our choices, and the most important decision we'll ever make is to accept Jesus Christ into our hearts and make Him the king of our lives. The only thing that will ever matter in Christians' lives is what they do to glorify Jesus. Those are the things that will last.

Put your treasures in heaven. There's going to be a time when everything this world has to offer you is a lie. Some of the things you face today are escapes—drugs, the party your friends are going to. Come on, guys! What's a party? You go out and you drink, and when you drink, you forget, and you're not yourself. That's an escape from a life you think isn't worth living. An escape from reality. When you lock yourself in your room, disappear into your music, and dream of being someone you're not, that's an escape. Put your lives in Jesus Christ. Those dreams and those parties lead nowhere but hell. Put your eyes on Jesus Christ.

For those of you who don't know Him, for those of you who haven't accepted Him into your hearts and made Him Lord of your life, think about it. Think about what matters. Think about things that are most important to you and ask yourself if they will still be important fifteen years from now. What will it matter when you die? Think about it.

At age nineteen and with barely ten months' experience of being physically handicapped, that was my message. I could speak about it because it was what the Lord had firmly impressed on my heart. Even so, I still became frustrated and fought to make my head knowledge real to my heart so that my doubts especially concerning His goodness would go away so I could be a "real Christian"— practically perfect in every way like Mary Poppins.

I knew all about the suggestive doubts that were whispered to me in the darkness when I lay there trying to sleep. Those lies were like cobwebs in the corners trying to encroach on territory that had been hard fought to win. It was a constant struggle not to give in to what I saw and felt in my physical reality and in the empty and hopeless world I observed around me that I could not explain or understand fully instead of believing in a God and His purposes unseen by me.

After I gave my talk before the camp audience, campers felt they knew me, and the invisible barrier came down as I became an accessible and safe person to talk to. I think God used those interactions probably more than my formal testimony. Some bared their souls and poured out their hurts while others just hung out with me.

I would leave on Tuesday evenings for Madison and return on Thursday evenings until the end of camp on Saturday. Then I would go home, attend church, eat lunch, and head back to camp on Sunday evening. I spent a lot of time alone driving my car across rural Wisconsin. I would sing at the top of my lungs, yell, cry, talk to myself, pray, and be silent. I had time to work through my experiences and struggles to make sense of my faith and how so much hurt fit into that equation.

I felt like the old tractor at my grandparents' that required you to practically stand on the clutch to shift gears; there was no way to change gears smoothly. It didn't grind because you hadn't put the gear in the way you should have; it just jerked and clacked as it changed to the new gear, and it did this no matter how smoothly you transitioned from clutch to gas. That's what my week felt like. For part of the week, I was in this concentrated Christian atmosphere at a camp with all these amazing people. Then I would try to prepare myself for the shift to a completely secular environment in which I desperately wanted to maintain, not compromise, my beliefs.

At camp, there was an openness to hear. At the hospital, my faith was received with an attitude of "Isn't that nice for you?" I struggled with that too. Was I doing something wrong or not being bold enough? To my knowledge, no one believed in Jesus because of me at the hospital. These were wonderful people I had grown to love and appreciate, so that broke my heart. Why couldn't they see that I was who I was not because I was a good person but because of my faith in Jesus and "Christ in me, the hope of glory." Of course, there were the continual disappointments I faced when there was no further progress with my prosthetics. I was overcome by emotion as I let them come out freely during these drives.

One evening after I came back to camp, I was particularly troubled and frustrated. Everyone had gone into the woods to play capture the flag, my favorite camp game, in the twilight. It was a mixture of tag, hide-and-seek, distraction, stealth, and speed to snatch your opponents' flag hidden somewhere in their territory and get it back to your territory. A game could last five minutes or five hours. I couldn't get close to where they were playing without help. I crawled into the trailer where I stayed while listening to voices drifting through the trees. I didn't turn on the light. I didn't climb onto my bed. I crawled into a dark corner and sat.

Those accusing, interior voices crawled out of the darkness—the truths of my pride, the lies that had been presented as questions since the dawn of time by the evil one. I gave up; I gave in as the sweet fumes of self-pity swirled around me. At first, it's like a drug, a release to be true to yourself, brutally honest. "Poor me" never felt so good. I didn't cry. I just let go. I did not check one thought. Before I knew it, I was drowning in it as it sucked me in deeper and deeper.

The darkness was palpable; it was physically becoming hard to breathe. I had never let go like that before. I just wanted to die. I was ready to die. Why had I been fighting it? I was being sucked down a black hole in that dark corner. I couldn't move. I didn't want to. I just wanted my life to end. I had not moved from the corner of the room, but I felt I was falling past despair into nothingness.

Then there was a quiet but clear voice: "Pam, this is not my plan for you." I felt too helpless to pray, just too far gone. Somewhere in me was enough strength to think if not say, *Help me.* Slowly, these words came into my head: "Jesus loves me this I know, for the Bible tells me so. Little ones to Him belong. They are weak, but He is strong."[10]

The words repeated in my head. They didn't swirl, question, or overwhelm me. They came slowly, confidently, compassionately. When they finally made it to my mouth, it took an excruciating amount of effort to whisper them into the darkness, but then it was like breathing fresh air again. I whispered them again more naturally, and my tears began to flow. It was a cleansing cry that began to wash away the putrid toxicity of the sin of selfish indulgence until finally I felt held. Invisible arms held me, and I sang. I have no idea how long all of that lasted. I know only that God saved me that evening … again.

Almost two decades later, I would hear Natalie Grant sing "Held" on the radio while I was driving. Facing another personal crisis, I had to pull over because I was sobbing. It brought me back to this moment of being held and reminded me as I was again facing loss and the unknown that God was faithful and was still holding me.

This Hand Is Bitterness

We want to taste it, let the hatred numb our sorrow
The wise hands opens slowly to lilies of the valley
and tomorrow

Chorus:
This is what it means to be held …
This is what it is to be loved
And to know that the promise was
When everything fell we'd be held.[11]

Being held in that moment, that meeting with God would be a "memorial stone" (Joshua 4), a place of remembrance that I would return to again and again when my strength was failing. Time and again, I would receive the same message: "My grace is sufficient for you." My calling is not even close to Paul's, but I did identify with his words.

> Therefore, in order to keep me from becoming conceited, I was given a thorn in my flesh, a messenger of Satan, to torment me. Three times I pleaded with the Lord to take it away from me. But he said to me, "My grace is sufficient for you, for my power is made perfect in weakness." Therefore I will boast all the more gladly about my weaknesses, so that Christ's power may rest on me. That is why, for Christ's sake, I delight in weaknesses, in insults, in hardships, in persecutions, in difficulties. For when I am weak, then I am strong. (2 Corinthians 12:7–10 NIV)

I knew these words were true, but the difficulty lay in remaining in Christ, keeping my eyes fixed on Jesus and not on the values of the world. The difficulty was and is in being content to put myself aside so I could live for Christ. I wanted to finally overcome the constant desire to fit in and find acceptance. I knew from experience that acceptance was always just out of reach. Its pursuit would lead anyone straight to the pit of hell literally and figuratively. Secularly, literary realism provides a plethora of heartbreaking examples of this in the genre's novels. Biblically, it's the lie that first deceived Eve, the one about self-importance and thinking we deserve better and more. Jesus addressed this in Luke 15 when He told the parable of the prodigal son and more poignantly the older brother, with whom I most identified. It is the insinuation that what I have right now is not good enough and that I will not be satisfied until I have more especially when I have worked so hard, suffered enough, done what

God asked, and so on. The discontentment that turns my head to look at others and ask God, "What about …?"

This lie leads straight into the next lie, which is that God is not good because He has the power to give me what I want or desire but does not, so according to my judgment, how could He be good? It is the reasoning of a petulant child. I was acting on my feelings in the moment instead of praying for the Holy Spirit's guidance and considering the motivations of my heart to recognize pride. If I forget to measure myself by the Word of God, my sense of self warps as I am twisted by the values around me. Slowly and subtly but surely, I usurp the place of God, which of course is exactly what Satan wants us to do.

Jesus wanted to show this rebellion against the Father in two ways through two sons. The prodigal was in his father's face with demands for his inheritance. Basically, he was telling his dad that he wished he were dead. This rebellion resulted in the father letting him have his way, and he abandoned his father. God also allows us to reject Him. He lovingly waits and longs for all prodigals to return. Whether they do or don't rests largely on their correct valuation of themselves in relation to God.

Meanwhile, the older brother worked religiously for the father while harboring the same rebellion his brother had. He preferred resentment to rejection. He felt that his father owed him something for his good behavior. Both sons failed to see the love of their father. Both felt they deserved more. Both failed to see that their riches and value were inexorably linked to being sons of their father, without whom they were nobodies who had nothing.

The prodigal experienced the love of his father because he accepted the love and restoration the father offered. The father also went out to find the faithful older brother in his misery as well. He offered him his love and reminded his son, "Everything I have is yours" (Luke 15:31 NIV). The older brother was so fixated on his brother's partying with his inheritance and his welcome-home party that he failed to see the father. I failed so often to keep my eyes on the Father, to look to Jesus because in Him I had all that really mattered.

I had prayed for my healing and restoration, and many others had offered prayers on my behalf as well, but there I sat in my wheelchair. That decision was not mine to make. The Lord promised me that He was enough. Would I believe Him? Would I look to Him as my loving Father, my loving Savior, the Holy Spirit who would guide, convict, comfort, and confirm me? I had a choice to make between life or death, blessing or cursing. Even at that time when not even a year had gone by, I knew that I would not exchange all that had happened to me even if I could have. I had learned and matured so much even though depression and discouragement nipped at me constantly. I knew the truth.

The following week, I was making my usual trip back from Madison and listening to a recording of the Reverend Dr. E. V. Hill. I had first heard the late Dr. Hill preach at the national convention our family had attended when I was in junior high. He had preached from Daniel 3 on Shadrach, Meshach, and Abednego in the fiery furnace. I was so moved by that sermon that I never have read Daniel 3 without Dr. Hill's words echoing in my mind. His message was that those who stood for God in times of trouble and compromise were the ones who had His attention.

> The eyes of the Lord are on the righteous, and his ears are attentive to their cry. (Psalm 34:15 NIV)

> For the eyes of the Lord range throughout the earth to strengthen those whose hearts are fully committed to him. (2 Chronicles 16:9a NIV)

I already had great respect for the preaching of this man of God, but the recording of this radio broadcast was different. Dr. Hill was preaching his wife's funeral. His pain and intensity were unmistakable as he remembered his wife, whom he called Baby.

He spoke about her amazing character as a woman and a wife. He recounted times of her support and selflessness such as the time she took the car for a drive after Dr. Hill had been threatened with a car bomb. Upon returning home, she quietly informed him that the car was safe.

Then Baby was diagnosed with cancer. The first time, the treatments were successful, and they praised the Lord for her healing, but a few years later, the cancer came back, and everyone prayed again for healing. Dr. Hill pleaded with the Lord not to take her, but the Lord took her to Himself.

I was listening to the recording on my car radio and picturing the tears streaming down his face as his voice broke and as if it were possible his tone intensified. I was crying for his loss. He was speaking so intimately about his conversation with God over his loss. His emotions were raw with grief as he yelled with pain, hope, and conviction concerning how God had answered him.

Then this godly man exhorted this same message to those who were listening. I was certain I shared this experience with many others who heard Dr. Hill on this occasion, but I heard God speaking directly to me. Dr. Hill spoke so honestly and passionately through his tears and grief what God had answered in response to his questions: "Trust Me! Trust Me! Trust Me!"[12]

Those words spoken through tears of profound grief—no, more like yelled in conviction—embodied for me the same kind of emotion I felt knowing the truth while my heart was broken and having no earthly idea how to move forward. I had to pull the car over then too because I was sobbing. How to summarize the gospel and discipleship in two words! There is nothing easy or simple about it, but the answer to this one question will make or break a life, a soul, a heart.

God asks us, "Will you trust Me?" I had to whisper yes through my sobs that late afternoon. Jesus's words to Peter in John 21:22 (NIV) echoed in my head from my essay I had read that past Christmas season on the living room floor. Jesus had responded to

Peter's inquiry about what would happen to John after he had heard his own fate with this: "What is that to you? Follow me." Like Peter, I could not compare my life to others' lives and judge the fairness of what God asked of me. He simply said, "Do you love Me? Then follow me. Trust Me." The whole question of faith in a nutshell is this: "Trust in the Lord with all your heart and lean not on your own understanding; in all your ways submit to him, and he will make your paths straight" (Proverbs 3:5–6 NIV).

In the solitude of my car, my resolution was firm. However, it was the how and the daily doing of trust that tripped me up. Trusting God would require a daily decision to be dependent on Him and take His Word as truth. Every day, I would have to honor my commitment to God's Word. But what I wanted was an easy one and done, a once-and-for-all decision with a happily-ever-after ending. I would make this decision and the Holy Spirit would just carry me through life like a leaf on the wind. Easy! Didn't Jesus say that His "yoke was easy" in Matthew 11:30 (NIV)? A yoke implies a burden to bear and work to be done. Jesus also said, "Whoever wants to be my disciple must *deny* themselves and take up their cross *daily* and follow me" (Luke 9:23 NIV; emphasis mine). It is a daily surrender to humbly submit to a yoke and deny myself, not a popular concept in our assertive culture. I had to deny myself when every media message outside the Bible assures me that without indulging my desires, I will never be happy. Popular voices in entertainment and psychology advise me to follow my heart. If I were to follow my heart, I doubt I would ever get out of bed. Being a disciple, a learner, of Jesus is not a question of feeling like one; it is a question of knowing and acting in a response of trust and love though a few more years passed before I began to understand that more deeply.

At age nineteen, my days were a roller-coaster of emotions that would take me up, down, around, and upside down depending on the circumstances. Some days, I didn't give God an outright no, but I didn't want to do, think, or feel anything. I wanted to avoid the question altogether, but the decision not to make a decision was my answer. "Not today. Today, I don't feel up to talking to or trusting You. I'm going to avoid You." It reminded me of Adam's and Eve's hiding in the garden.

I have been guilty of putting Jesus on pause, on hold—my passive-aggressive response to maintain my false sense of control. I didn't reject God, but I didn't submit to Him either. I wanted wiggle room so I could have things my way. The result was that the question of trust remained an open one that was far deeper than I had considered and more difficult. Trusting God was a challenge as He asked for the uncomfortable, unattractive, and impossible when I looked forward to the rest of my life.

Take for example Romans 8:28 (NIV): "And we know that in all things God works for the good of those who love him, who have been called according to his purpose." This verse made my whole body tense up due to the way it was thrown at me from albeit well-intentioned people. The part that offended me so much was the flippant way someone would quote it as if that verse were the answer to all my problems so I should feel so much better. But truth be told, it is the answer. I want to think that anyone who has suffered loss in this life would never slap it on a person in an attempt to comfort them without a lot more context. To throw out this verse carelessly to someone who is hurting is comparable to using a Band-Aid to close an incision after open-heart surgery.

The testing of our faith proves our faith, and that testing in whatever form it takes is never easy. To lessen the gravity, pain, fear, etc. and the time required to learn the from the lessons and discipline (learning) of God in our lives is to cheapen faith. The verses in the context of Romans 8 convey how the Holy Spirit helps us in our weakness and suffering; without His help, I would have given in to despair. Listening to Dr. Hill's message and manner confirmed both—the pain and the faith that our God is worthy of our trust.

Looking back on how slowly I was to hold on to what is more second nature to me now has given me patience to pray and grace to accept God's timing and working in myself and others. More important, it has made me grateful. The Lord works with faith the size of a mustard seed patiently, faithfully, and with great love. "Thus far the Lord has helped us" (1 Samuel 7:12 NIV) is true in my life. I observe the years that have passed and see God's faithful presence in my life. "For you, God, tested us; you refined us like silver" (Psalm 66:10 NIV). Silver is refined by being heated to the point that any impurities in it are burned off; the process requires the refiner's vigilance. Of course, it is a metaphor for us to better understand suffering. The Lord said, "See, I have refined you, though not as silver; I have tested you in the furnace of affliction" (Isaiah 48:10 NIV). To remember these events is to remember that He is always present and in control.

In addition to all the ways that God showed Himself to me that summer at camp, He provided an experience that would better equip me to face the days ahead. I had the privilege of meeting Dr. Joseph Stowell, who at the time was the president of Moody Bible Institute. He had just completed a book, *Through the Fire*. He graciously gave me a copy that he personally dedicated to me with verses from Isaiah 43.

> But now, this is what the Lord says—he who created you, Jacob, he who formed you, Israel: "Do not fear, for I have redeemed you; I have summoned you by name; you are mine. When you pass through the waters, I will be with you; and when you pass through the rivers, they will not sweep over you. When you walk through the fire, you will not be burned; the flames will not set you ablaze. For I am the Lord your God, the Holy One of Israel, your Savior." (Isaiah 43:1–3a NIV)

Once again, a reminder of the promise that God was there and that when trouble came, He promised Himself, His presence.

CHAPTER 9

Returning

The long days of summer began to shorten. In Wisconsin, August evenings hinted at the cool that was autumn's forerunner. My time at the camp was over as was my time at the hospital. That amazing summer, I had learned so much and had been blessed by so many people who encouraged me.

August stretched like a long shadow before me marking the one-year anniversary since I got sick, had my birthday, and lost my legs. My thoughts kept drifting to where I had been and what I had been doing a year earlier. Ironically, that August, I was going to St. Louis as we should have a year earlier but for a different reason. Sara and Ricardo were getting married. I was going as her maid of honor. My brother went with me; it was an opportunity for the two of us to talk on the road.

Antonio was supposed to have come to the wedding, but I selfishly didn't want to see him; he had heard that, so he graciously didn't attend. Determined to walk down the aisle and sit only on a stool in front, I ended up tearing my skin, but I figured it was worth it.

I was happy for Sara, but it was emotionally and physically difficult for me. I put my best face forward as well as I could. Memories and the what-ifs kept rolling me over and over like a piece of driftwood caught in the surf. I was especially thankful that Eric was with me for the drive home so my mind wouldn't wander where it shouldn't have. Eric was about to begin his senior year in high school. We talked about everything—the church, music, and so on during our eleven-hour trip home.

A few weeks later, I returned to Grace College via one last stop for my final hospital follow-up. After that, my appointments would happen at the prosthetist's office. My parents were going with me to help me move in. They set up a ramp, bought a compact washer and dryer, and handled many other details to help me live independently; most of these were purchased with the money I received as a gift from the camp. It was difficult, but for the first time in a long time, I felt I was moving forward.

I lived off campus to accommodate my situation in the wheelchair. I was back in the formerly familiar but at that point strange place. What I found most difficult was the loss of my sense of belonging that had been based on activities I had participated in. I wanted to be normal, but that was something I had never felt anyway, so why I was still stuck on that I had no idea. The cold, hard facts of my physical condition made me different and dependent on others and made me feel I was on display. Helping someone out short term is OK, but giving long-term help drains people. I ended up being permanently excused from chapel because it was just too difficult to get long-term volunteers to get me up and down the stairs. After a few too many times of waiting on the upper landing until I knew chapel had begun, the emotional turmoil was just too much along with everything else. It was no one's fault. There was no one to blame, but I still felt humiliated, rejected, and left out of one more activity. Any sense of community I had had before was lost, and many of the people I had known there had graduated the year before.

Even so, as homecoming approached that autumn, someone who probably didn't know me very well nominated me for homecoming queen. On first thought, I was flattered; on second thought, I was mortified. I tried to explain this to some people but gave up trying.

I kept being told I had been nominated for all the right reasons, which made me feel that I could not and should not disappoint by insisting my name be removed, which would have been so much easier for so many reasons.

I had to face the consequences of this nomination, but my stomach and head ached due to my anxiety about it. Having just been in a wedding party a couple months before, I knew I had to get the dress fitted. I had been determined to walk even though my skin had torn badly. Finally, the worst obstacle of all—shoes! Shoes were a problem because they had to have the perfect tennis shoe heel height in a dress shoe and they could not be slip-ons. In conclusion, my only choice was ugly shoes. And even those were almost impossible to find. I imagined the look on people's faces as a legless young woman in a wheelchair searched for shoes; I couldn't look for fear of laughing or crying.

At the wedding, I had had to lean on the guy walking down the aisle with me, which meant I had to touch him with my deformed hands, and to top it all off, I had to smile even though I was in pain and perspiring profusely. Because of this wedding experience, I faced homecoming with growing apprehension. I knew what barriers I faced at the auditorium, where I would have to go up and down five steps to get on and off the stage. Besides that, I had to find a date so I'd have a guy I could lean on. These thoughts brought Antonio to my mind. He would have been Ricardo's best man at their wedding, but I had told Sara that I couldn't face him and that if he came, I couldn't and wouldn't go. Reflecting on that, I was so ashamed. I was also alone. I knew next to no one. Those I did know were going with their girlfriends. I asked friends I had made at camp, but they were far away, which was very unfair of me. But finally, a friend of a friend graciously agreed to go with me.

Then I moved on to the practical solutions to wardrobe issues. The chosen court dress was too short for me and showed the neoprene sleeves that held my prosthetics on. Though I had normal prosthetics for a below-knee amputee at that time, they still affected my wardrobe choices. The hard-composite material that fit my stumps was held in place with neoprene suspension sleeves (think wet-suit material) that extended a few inches below my knee on the outside of the composite and rolled up my thigh. The sleeve was about eighteen inches tall. My prosthetics had a cosmetic cover to give the legs a supposedly realistic look and hide the titanium bar that attached with the assistance of specialty hardware to the foot and the hard, stump-shaped composite.

So my elegant dress wouldn't look right unless it was much longer. I had to find someone who could alter and add to the delicate fabric. A friend from my church helped me find a seamstress who could do that. The dress chosen for the homecoming court would look spectacular on the young woman usually nominated for these things. I on the other hand felt like a hippopotamus on stilts. I was thankful for the long black gloves that hid my hands and the scars on my wrists. Stuffing Kleenex in missing finger places helped a little, but the gloves still flopped awkwardly.

The night finally came, and I thought I was ready though I was almost unbearably nervous. I was crowned queen and smiled as valiantly as I could while I was dying inside. The physical pain was intense. I couldn't wait to get back to my wheelchair, but I kept smiling. Then after my less than graceful descent off the stage, we attended a formal dinner in the transformed school cafeteria. I hadn't been there for almost a year. It was strange to be there again, and I was flooded with memories. I had to stay in the present and keep smiling.

Eating was still a challenge for me. Much like a toddler, I preferred finger foods. I still had reduced feeling in my remaining fingers, so using a fork and knife was awkward on my best days, and I was extremely self-conscious about the way my hands looked. As the food was brought to the table, the other ladies of the homecoming court removed their long, black gloves. I did as well and tried to pull myself together as the lump of rising emotion grew in my throat and chest. Meanwhile, the perfectly manicured and jeweled hands of the other ladies of the homecoming court moved gracefully and seemingly at ease in this social setting of the couples of students, faculty, and alumni. I was beyond uncomfortable. I was counting down the minutes before I could escape. I couldn't make small talk with anyone; not a single cell of my being belonged in the tuxedo and formal gown gathering.

Leaving as quickly as possible, I thanked my date, went home, slammed the door to my room awkwardly, and threw the crown in my closet before I cried myself to sleep. The crown stayed in the closet for quite some time before I was able to look at it again. I wanted to throw it away many times, but I have it to this day as a glittery reminder of the shame of my vanity and the humiliation associated with keeping up with the appearance and expectations of others.

Many painful lessons lay ahead, ones I thought I'd learned, but no. My pride was still inexplicably intact in ways that made my negative personality hypercritical of others. I tired of people's stares at my stumps as I sat in my wheelchair though I was fond of saying that if people were going to stare, I'd give them something to stare at. And then I'd stick where one of the nubs of my amputated fingers in a nostril which gave the impression that my finger was impossibly up my nose. Of course, this was only done for friends to back up my bluster.

I was feeling sorry for myself at a McDonald's in Chicago when everyone's attention was drawn to a large, obese patron walking in. There might as well have been a tap on my shoulder and somebody saying, "Excuse me, Pam. I believe you find such staring offensive." Talk about being a hypocrite. If I couldn't live up to my own expectations, how could I expect others to? I had so many foot-in-mouth experiences that I just wanted to drop off the face of the earth figuratively and literally.

Those thoughts came too. Every time I picked up one particular serrated kitchen knife, I was tempted to use it and not for food prep. One time I took it to the bathroom with me and started the warm water in the tub, but I remembered my summer camp experience. I sat on a towel draped over the seat and the back of the wheelchair and covered myself with another by holding it up with my teeth. I took the knife back to the kitchen and dropped it back into its drawer. I thought about throwing that knife out too. Unfortunately, the problem wasn't the knife. It was me. I still have the knife as a reminder of my victory over the temptation of embracing death as an escape.

My roommate and I were living in a house that was next to campus and close to the library, where my English classes were held. It had three bedrooms upstairs, a large living room, a formal dining room, a kitchen, and an informal dining area. The basement, which was half-underground, was another rental with a different entrance. The number of renters in our place increased as we tried to accommodate others in their hour of need, but before long, misunderstandings and a lack of privacy put a great deal of strain even on good relationships. We were young and had good intentions, but we lacked the necessary boundaries to maintain good relationships.

Six of us lived in different areas of the house at one time, and I changed my living space there three times that year. The disadvantage of renting half of the house with no garage was that we all had to park on the street. My parallel parking skills were honed during that school year. I parked right in front of the house so that my passenger door opened directly onto the walk that led to it; there wasn't a sidewalk on our street. Many times I got stuck. Many times I cried in frustration. Frustration because I hated being trapped by my body and irritation that I actually had to make a case for myself and be a whiner and a complainer. I hated being so needy that I had to ask for certain things. Relations became tense; I preferred to simply avoid the conflict. That didn't mean it went away though; it just ate me alive from inside, where I had stuffed it.

I decided to live alone the next year. I was perhaps finally growing up. I had been too afraid before, but I was more than ready at that point. My insecurity had nothing to do with my physical handicap. I would not go to any social situation on my own. If I hadn't had anyone to sit with in the cafeteria during my freshman year, I hadn't gone.

Since my return to college, almost all my friends were new; to them, I had always been disabled. I attended the same Hispanic church, but I no longer walked to Nancy's house with my problems like I had done before getting sick. When I had been with Antonio, I wanted to know all about how Nancy and Mario had made their intercultural, interracial relationship work because I had been told that most marriages like that didn't make it past five years. They had been together for twenty years with a son in high school and two other children in elementary school. I used to just spend time at their house until I had to let them sleep. It was very selfish of me, but I loved how open they were, and there was always food for me and many others who stopped by. I learned about openness and hospitality from Nancy. She didn't put on airs; she didn't have the time. It didn't matter if the floors were clean or dirty, her door was open. Her door was still open, but I didn't go in. Her house was a reminder of a different life.

I made friends with new people and hung out mostly in different places. One new friend I met at the Spanish-speaking church had grown up in Spain as a missionary kid. Over Christmas and winter break, she was body slammed by an out-of-control skier on a ski slope back home in Colorado. She was in a cast up to her thigh after a knee surgery, and I had given her my bedroom in our rental. She also attended the Hispanic church with me and other missionary kids who spoke Spanish. I accompanied them to another couple's house, an American woman married to an Argentine man. They had three preschool boys who were just adorable, and their door was always open too. Pablo and Lynette's house was filled with love, laughter and music. I watched Lynette with those boys, and she was pregnant with their fourth, and I marveled at how she handled motherhood. I loved how she gently interacted with her rambunctious boys. I was on the floor much of the time anyway since there was really no room or need for the wheelchair in their small, two-bedroom house. I found that nothing melted the cares of the world away like playing and laughing with children. I found a refuge in their home, the same as I had in Nancy's home before but with different needs, or so I thought.

One day that winter, Nancy stopped me at church. She sat with me and expressed how much she missed me. She told me how proud she was of my faith and determination. Then she said something that stung my pride and pierced my heart. She told me how much she loved me and that she felt as if I'd left her behind. That was true. I had left behind most of the people I had been close to before I got sick. I had been so determined to move forward that I had decided not to look back, but Nancy challenged me. If I wanted to have peace and complete healing, I needed to have the courage to look back and face the people I knew and the dreams I had before my disability that I was avoiding because they were too painful to revisit. I would have to place them before God and have the courage to renew those relationships and dreams or to honestly and lovingly close those chapters of my life.

She encouraged me to evaluate what kept me from her home and what had stopped me from having contact with the people who had loved me and prayed for me in Spain, and that included Antonio. She gently but firmly continued as I fought back tears. "For the Spirit God gave us does not make us timid, but gives us power, love and self-discipline" (2 Timothy 1:7 NIV). I realized I needed to ask God for the power and love to overcome the fear and shame of facing my past. I recognized the value and love of the people who were with me before and my need to embrace them with gratitude even if only to be able to say thank you and say healthy goodbyes. We were crying as she prayed for me. I didn't want to think about what she had said; I tried to justify myself, but questions nagged at me between wakefulness and sleeping, and in my heart, I knew she was right.

Ever so slowly and painfully, I began walking more and more. Nothing consistent, but walking. I also started doing things beyond my classes such as keeping stats for the basketball team. I had done that in high school, and it was fun. I made good friends and enjoyed long conversations about idealistic plans and solving the world's problems on bus rides to and from school on away games. Wearing my legs helped me feel more normal. The basketball players ignored me unless they thought I had messed something up with their statistics, which was also a normal response. Best of all, my friends accepted me as normal. Normal!

My grades were better than ever; not working two jobs helped a great deal when it came to school. I had had a Brother typewriter that allowed for corrections up to twelve characters for school papers; it was outstanding. (I realize some of you have no idea what I'm talking about, or what footnotes are, or how you had to turn the wheel ever so slightly to make footnote numbers appear properly. A student's life was hard. No Google; just the library card catalogue and good luck!)

I had been able to type fairly well thanks to a business typing class in high school. One of the benefits I received through the vocational education program at the hospital was a word processor. Not a computer, just a word processor that allowed me to save documents to those big, four-inch by four-inch floppy discs and print them out on a matrix dot printer. It did not have spell check or any of those things, but it did allow me to revise my writing and typing errors due to my missing fingers.

I was feeling more comfortable with my new normal. Frustrations still popped up, but I was determined to overcome my obstacles. Winter in Indiana was a formidable obstacle. My wheels were always wet from rain, snow, or slush. Early morning classes often meant that snow had not been cleared as I forged through a layer of the stuff. My jeans were wet from the wheels from late December to early April. Inevitably, my pants would nearly have dried when it was time to venture out again.

Once when it was super icy, I could not get my wheelchair up the ramp to the front door of our rental house. The wheels would spin, and I would slide back down sideways. I was glad there was a little lip on the edges of my homemade ramp or I would have slid off the side. After a few attempts, I got down from the wheelchair and pulled it up the ramp behind me. I was freezing and soaked to the bone by the time I finally made it into the house.

The only falls I had in my prosthetics were on ice. My feet would just slide apart, and I was powerless to stop that; I had no recourse but to fall over sideways, crawl over to a patch of snow, and try to stand. It took me about half an hour to figure out how to get up again and do it. If I could get near a tree or car or crawl to someone's front steps, I was guaranteed success. If I was in an open area, I thought someone would eventually find my frozen body. Seriously though, I would finally manage to get the angle just so to get myself off the ground; it took a lot of prayer and repeated attempts.

At that time, 80 percent of my life was spent in my wheelchair compared to 20 percent using prosthetics independently. Situations like these were all within the range of normal as well, but I still insisted on being independent. I would get parked in because someone would leave a shopping cart, motorcycle, or bicycle in the yellow lines next to my handicapped space so I could not open my door wide enough to get in or out. I learned that apparently some people could not see the lines from inside their motor vehicles either. When I was in my wheelchair, I was able to crawl to the door, squeeze in, and slide into the driver's seat and then back out enough to open the door completely to load my wheelchair and groceries in and go home. If I was wearing my prosthetics however, I was stuck if the object blocking my door was not moveable. I would have to wait until the driver arrived and moved his or her vehicle so I could open the door wide enough to get my unbendable legs in.

My preference was to say nothing because I'd somehow end up to blame for my predicament when I dared mentioning something. I even had people tell me that I was not handicapped. An elderly gentleman screamed obscenities at me one day for parking in a handicapped spot without the plastic handicap decal that hangs from the rearview mirror. My license plates bore the wheelchair symbol, but he continued to insult me as I rolled away, legless, in my wheelchair. I learned to breathe deeply. I learned to wait.

It was a good thing I still carried this inscribed on my keychain.

But they who *wait* for the Lord shall renew their strength; they shall mount up with wings like eagles; they shall run and not be weary; they shall walk and not faint. (Isaiah 40:31 KJV; emphasis mine)

I had tantrums, meltdowns, and bad days; the warning signs would be the look on my face or how the sarcasm would drip from my lips. I also knew that God had allowed me to live like this and that none of these circumstances escaped His notice. I knew that I had enough potential venom in me to poison myself and everyone around me with bitterness or that I could ask God to forgive me and help me, forgiveness because Ephesians 4:32 (NIV) says, "Be kind and compassionate to one another, forgiving each other, just as in Christ God forgave you." And I asked Him for help because there was no way I was going to make it without it. Some days, it was all I could do to struggle out of my dirty and sometimes wet pants and curl up in the fetal position under my covers. I read my Bible and copied the verses that spoke to me, you know, the ones that jumped off the page because they comforted, convicted, or inspired me.

Some days, I wrote out my thoughts before God because my mind and emotions were twisted and knotted as if fifty kittens had been turned loose on a ball of yarn while trapped in a box for eight hours. I would be so tangled up inside that I couldn't think straight. Writing helped me grab a loose end and start to untangle my heart and mind. God was faithful in giving me verses and memories as I wrote that encouraged me. I wrote this passage on a notecard and put it on my bathroom mirror.

> Teach me your way, Lord, that I may rely on your faithfulness; give me an undivided heart, that I may fear your name. I will praise you, Lord my God, with all my heart; I will glorify your name forever. For great is your love toward me; you have delivered me from the depths, from the realm of the dead. (Psalm 86:11–13 NIV)

I read books by Corrie ten Boon, Elizabeth Elliot, and yes, Joni Eareckson. I repeatedly thanked God for them. Their experiences helped lead me through mine. All three had lived through much more difficult circumstances than mine, and their words were valuable to me as they pointed me to Jesus.

Shadow of the Almighty by Elizabeth Elliot is a biography of sorts about her late husband, Jim Elliot, in which she shares his journal writings and letters. They had spent long periods apart during their courtship. (Using the word *dating* for Jim and Bette just doesn't seem correct.) Since Antonio and I had written letters for seven months, I felt a certain connection to them as they wrote about their circumstances, but they were always bringing their concerns back to the Bible and centering their thoughts on God's providence and purpose. I wrote out several quotes, passages, and prayers of theirs that encouraged me and resonated in my heart. Jim wrote, "Remember Marah. 'And the LORD showed him (Moses) a tree, which, when he had cast into the waters, the waters were made sweet.' The cloud *led* Israel to Marah (emphasis mine). "[13]

I copied that in my journal. Marah means bitterness; the water there tasted so terrible that it was undrinkable even in a desert dying of thirst. God had led them there without explanation, and the people complained as per usual; it's what people do. But Moses prayed as per usual; that makes all the difference.

Ever since Nancy had challenged me, I had been praying especially when it came to Spain but in particular about Antonio. It was as if Nancy had opened a closet door where I had stuffed too much in and now it all lay there scattered across the floor. There was no easy way to pick up everything and get the door closed on it again. I needed to deal with it first, but I didn't know how. I had been conflicted about calling Antonio; I did not want to act on impulse and open an old wound; I wanted to find healing for a wound that would not close all the way. I prayed. A lot.

On our weekly long-distance phone call (no cell phones or texting back then), my parents had told me a female had called and asked for me in Spanish. Then Sara and Ricardo called to reschedule a visit and said that things were happening with Antonio. I dared to ask what, but Ricardo evenly told me that if I wanted to know, I should ask Antonio directly. I wondered if the call to my parents had been from Mari-Carmen, Antonio's sister. I knew that God had allowed and had led me—us—to this circumstance. I wondered if God was showing me a sweet way out of my bitterness. I prayed some more though I knew what I wanted to do.

I broke my own rules and called Spain for the first time since I had been sick. I was so nervous that I was nauseous. Mari-Carmen answered and said immediately on recognizing my voice, "Pamela! Antonio! Es Pamela!" Before I could get a word in, I heard Antonio's voice. I was shaking, but I was polite as we spoke. I remember nothing about that conversation; my diary said simply, "We had a wonderful time."

Though it was a cold winter day, the ice around that part of my heart cracked. Then the planned weekend arrived when Sara and Ricardo drove up from St. Louis for a visit. In a rare moment, it was just the three of us in the house, and there were three phones in the house. (One bathroom but three phones.) We had been laughing and reminiscing about our time in Spain. We decided to call Antonio, but he wasn't home, so we talked to his mom for a while. We called later as instructed, and we all talked and laughed.

Then Ricardo and Sara left the two of us talking as they had previously schemed. I found myself on the verge of tears because of Antonio's kindness; I knew I had done nothing to deserve it. I had cut him off; he had had no word from me in over a year. He had missed being Ricardo's best man at the wedding because of me. He didn't demand explanations or reproach me when at the bare minimum I probably deserved a tongue lashing. I told him I would send him a picture of me with the artificial legs. He quietly asked why I hadn't done that before. I told him I had changed. He told me that he thought of me as he always had. I repeated that I had changed. My diary entry reads at the end, "I am so confused."

But this part I do remember clearly—how wonderful it was to be loved and accepted by someone who found me special. On the other hand, I knew how messed up I was physically and emotionally, and I had no desire to hurt or be hurt again. I could not deny my feelings for Antonio for all the reasons I had had them before, but my feelings were not to be trusted. Even so, it was becoming apparent that I needed to make a decision about facing this so I could move forward. I had already opened the door to Antonio if only in friendship; the unresolved needed to be resolved. Proverbs 16:1–3 (NIV) echoed that.

> To humans belong the plans of the heart, but from the Lord comes the proper answer of the tongue. All a person's ways seem pure to them, but motives are weighed by the Lord. Commit to the Lord whatever you do, and he will establish your plans.

I like how the Living Bible puts the same passage.

> We can make our plans, but the final outcome is in God's hands. We can always "prove" that we are right, but is the Lord convinced? Commit your work to the Lord, then it will succeed.

Waiting for some clarity about doing what was right was difficult because my emotions were in flux. A million and one thoughts and questions swirled in my mind anytime I was still enough, and then my mind would just not turn off. I wrote out my prayers and then destroyed them; I was too ashamed to imagine that someone might read them as I poured out every dark thought about my motivations before God. I thought about my parents and questioned if my illness had been God's discipline for not honoring my parents on the subject of Antonio. I knew well that my parents were the safety net below my precarious tightrope of independence. I wanted to be truly independent, and my parents respected that, but they were the ones who had made possible what I had emotionally and financially. I managed my own affairs for the most part financial and otherwise, but the remainder was significant and would have caused the abysmal failure of my quick ascent back to independence had my parents filled in the spaces and cracks I could not.

I did not tell my parents that I had made contact with Antonio, and I knew that omission was telling. Worse, I could convince myself both ways, both for and against a return to Spain. I reread my journals from when I had gone to Spain and began dating Antonio. I remembered my midnight walks and prayers around the lake before I had gone to Spain in the first place and how I had poured my heart out to God begging Him to give me a clear direction in my life and how He had answered. I remembered how those questions resolved in a clear direction only to be led to Marah, to bitterness. I continued to pray; what else could I do? I had no idea what to do with these thoughts. The next excerpt from *Shadow of the Almighty* in my diary was from the end of the following chapter.

Remember that we have bargained with Him who bore a cross, and in His ministry to those disciples His emphasis was upon sacrifice, not of worldly goods so much as of family ties. Let nothing turn us from the truth that God has determined that we

become strong under fire, after the pattern of the
Son. Nothing else will do. Our silken selves must
know denial. Hear Amy Carmichael [missionary to
India; topic of another of E. Elliot's books, *A Chance
to Die*]: O Prince of Glory, Who dost bring Thy sons
to glory through the Cross. Let us not shrink back
from suffering, reproach or loss.[14]

I made lists under those headings—suffering, reproach, and
loss—but I was still at a loss as to what I should do except for one
thing. I needed to wait to hear from God.

Until then, I continued to read His Word and study to complete
my degree in secondary English and Spanish education and to
pursue student teaching in both. I knew who my supervising
Spanish teacher would be as she had vetted my Spanish and made
an exception to take me on as a student teacher. I had volunteered
in community workshops with her to teach Spanish before I had lost
my legs. I was unclear with whom I would teach English and how
that would fit together.

My day-to-day life was going on as it had when I received a
call from Sara; they were going to Spain that summer, and they
wondered if I would like to travel with them. That made me more
excited and frustrated. I told the Lord that I needed a clear direction
because this was an opportunity or a temptation—I wasn't sure
which; I argued both sides. I sobbed, and I begged God to give me
a sign.

The following morning, I entered the classroom for my 7:30
Modern American Grammar class, and there on the chalkboard,
a Spanish verb in the present tense was conjugated. I sat in that
classroom several times a week; it was an English Department
classroom where we diagrammed sentences and drew out plot lines,
but never in all my time in that room had there ever been any modern
foreign language on the board. Old English lines from *Beowulf*, yes,
the occasional Latin or Greek root of an English term, but never

anything else. Also, the chalkboards were impeccably black at 7:30 in the morning having been wiped down after evening classes, but not that morning. I read the conjugation of a Spanish verb.

voy   vamos
vas   vais
va   van

It was *ir*, the verb "to go" in Spanish right before my eyes. I almost started to cry. I was the most excited I had ever been at 7:30 in the morning in my Modern American Grammar class. I thanked God over and over.

When I knew the dates and the airline, I called my parents. There was no resistance or trying to talk me out of it; they accepted what I was saying as if it were inevitable and that they had just been waiting for the when. I called Antonio and told him that I was just his friend but that I needed to face Spain in my wheelchair. I also wanted him and everyone else to see that I was OK.

I finished the school year and went home for my last summer there. My brother had graduated from high school and was heading to LeTourneau University in Texas in the fall. My parents had decided it was time for them to move back to Arizona for their aching joints. Every winter in Wisconsin became increasingly more painful for them due to the lingering effects of the major car accident we had been in when I was four. They had waited until Eric had finished high school to make this move. My father had accepted a position back at the main church in Chandler that he had worked under before.

Change was coming. I wasn't sure what would become of me, but I had a trip coming up and another year of college before I had to think long term so I wasn't bothered, just nostalgic knowing that home would be quite different after that summer.

In the end, it was just me going to Spain for five weeks since Sara and Ricardo had to postpone their trip. Plans had been made for me to attend a church camp in Spain where I would give my testimony almost right away. I was glad to get a chance to speak to everyone about what had happened. I could speak to groups without a flood of emotions, but when I spoke one on one, I was much more vulnerable and let my emotions show.

I repeated to Antonio that I was just a friend now, just a friend. It was the first time I was flying since I had become disabled, so it was more of an adventure, but I was confident I could make it work. I wore my legs to get on and off the plane and to the bathroom, but off the plane, I used my wheelchair. I wore a skirt so that I could remove my legs during the flight so my skin would not break down so quickly from the stress of that long flight. Between the blanket and my full skirt, I don't think anyone even noticed.

I wanted to meet everyone walking, so right before I went out the door after finishing passport and customs controls, I thanked the airport assistant and stood as we placed my bags on the wheelchair so I could push it as I walked out into the waiting area.

I was blown away by everyone who had come to the airport. Antonio's whole family was there as were our friends from church. Antonio stood off to the side holding flowers. I'm not sure if what I had said about our being just friends lasted even five minutes in my heart. Despite the wheelchair and silent, painful months that had passed, it was as if everything picked up from the same moment we had been at two summers previously.

I started out staying with a missionary in Móstoles, where Antonio helped with the church there, and then with Ricardo's brother and wife in Alcalá de Henares, the city where Antonio lived. This had been part of the original plan with Sara and Ricardo because they had an apartment on the ground floor.

After the first two weeks, I started being able to walk every day for the first time. My skin was holding up; I almost dared to hope. The month was flying by as we started at church camp and then visiting friends and receiving visitors. I stayed with Antonio and his family for the last two weeks. I walked up the four floors of stairs to his family's apartment. It was like coming home.

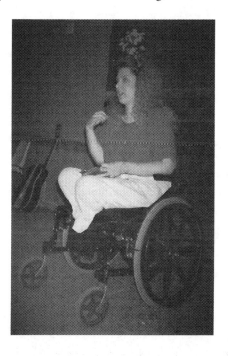

Speaking at the summer camp in Spain, 1990

By that time, Antonio and I had taken our relationship as seriously as we had two summers earlier, but before making anything official, I told him he had to see me first because I was in my words deformed. (The politically correct term is that I experienced limb difference.) He said it didn't matter, but I knew how badly scarred I was. I didn't like looking at my legs, so how could he? I sat on the bottom bunk in the room Mari-Carmen and I shared and stripped down so he could see what was left of my legs. I fought back tears as he kneeled in front of me. Tears spilled over as he kissed my scars telling me over and over that it changed nothing for him and that he loved me. When I was with Antonio, I almost believed I was beautiful again.

We set the date for getting married the next summer in Spain. I wanted my family to see me there and know I was being taken care of and loved. Mari-Carmen was the sister I never had. My favorite memory was staying up and talking until she jumped up and asked if I wanted to eat something. She came back with a chunk of good Spanish bread and a huge bar of milk chocolate to make a sandwich. I just laughed and told her I gained five kilos just watching her eat that!

I also learned something about my parents that summer. My parents had really *seen* Antonio when I was in the hospital, and they had all shared a room for over a month. Our prayers about that had been answered. My dad had written him and given him updates on what was happening with me because he felt it was only fair to Antonio to let him know. I had had no idea.

The previous two years had been a time of questioning and growing for Antonio also. His journey of faith could fill another book. As I had been at camp the summer before, he had spent his vacation on a mission trip with Operation Mobilization. Young people from all over the world came together and went out in teams to different locations. In his case, the meeting place was Offenburg, Germany, and then they worked with a church in Valladolid, Spain.

His plans had been demolished when I got sick and again when I broke off our engagement. He had also prayed and was sure that I had been the one when he had asked me to marry him two years earlier. During this time, he wrestled with God in his own way until one evening he clearly understood that the Lord wanted him to release his thoughts of me and unconditionally trust Him.

We had been an ocean apart, but God had brought us to the place where we surrendered everything and everyone into His divine care. Without any answers or guarantees of anything except His presence, we had separately made the decision to trust Him on a level that was deeper than we had known existed when we had prayed together on the shore of Lake Superior. As we sat on the balcony floor after the sun went down trying to catch a cool breeze in the heat of

August and some just-the-two-of-us moments, we tried to imagine the future. We knew how fragile plans could be. We were uncertain if we could have children and many other things, but we knew God would be with us, and His love bound our hearts.

When I came back to the States, most of the house I had called home was packed up; there were things for me to sort through. There were many tearful goodbyes especially with my dear Miss Ruth, who was at that point living with a sister because she couldn't be on her own anymore.

On my last night at the place that had been home in Greenwood, we sat outside on the patio that connected the parsonage to the church. The sky was filled with an amazing display of the northern lights. I have never seen them as clearly or as brightly again. The glowing green curtain of lights waved as if to say goodbye. I thanked God for this display and His faithfulness as the curtain closed on that part of my life.

My parents and brother drove with me in a caravan of two cars and the van with a long trailer. I was renting an unfurnished basement apartment with a sheltered parking area so I would be more protected from rain and snow. The driveway was a long, private easement that had a small loop at the end where the house was. Snow removal was taken care of by the owners. The door opened into a finished basement kitchen. There was a large window over the sink, but then the ground sloped up so that three-quarters of the apartment was underground with only wheel-well windows. It was perfect for me. The stairwell in the center of the apartment was closed off. The quadrants divided equally from that point: kitchen, living area, bedroom, and a combined bathroom, laundry, and utility room. I would be using some furniture that would not fit in my mom's and dad's much smaller Arizona home, but the majority of my things had been in storage.

They helped me set everything up. Pablo and Lynette came over while the boys played in the yard. Lynette was pregnant with their fourth child. I had joked that Lynette should wait until my birthday, which was much later than her due date. Well, a beautiful little girl came on my birthday, which was now hers too! After the celebrations, the shorter caravan continued on toward Texas with a final stop in Arizona.

I lived alone in that basement apartment, but I was not alone. My life was filled with people, purpose, and peace—not perfection or the absence of trouble or trials, but just the peace of knowing God more deeply, having much more compassion for people around me, and having gained more wisdom. I had the peace that comes from trusting that God holds everything in His hands and of releasing the what-ifs of the past and future more easily; one is regret and the other is fear existing in the realm of fantasy. Reality and truth are God's domain; if the what-ifs ever came to be in the future, God would meet me there just as He had guided what was in the past. Each day requires an honest assessment of what is and how to live there. God's grace had been sufficient for me, and I chose to believe Him that it would always be sufficient. I felt hope for the future. I anticipated being a bride and finding my place in the world because of God's grace. I lived to the fullest knowing this was my last year in this place with these people I had grown to love and who had taught me so much about love and living day by day.

I was able to complete my student-teaching assignment standing except for one day when I wasn't able to wear my prosthetics. I loved my supervising teachers and learned more about the art of teaching than I had known. I was critiqued and encouraged honestly, which helped me improve. I was blessed with thoughtful conversations exploring the philosophy, research, and personal experience of master teachers. I developed the principles that guided my teaching style, methods, and personal practices from this time.

At Christmastime, I flew to Arizona to be with my parents. A couple of days later, Antonio joined me. Eric arrived by car. We laughed as we planned our wedding in Spain. We crafted announcements and invitations in English and Spanish. We decided that my dad and the missionary who had mentored Antonio would perform the service in English and Spanish.

I had to worry about my dress and simple decorations while Antonio finalized arrangements for the restaurant and photographer. Back then, weddings were not as complicated as they seem to be today, and I was all for keeping things simple. There were aspects of the wedding in Spain that would be different; for example, we would be married by a judge to make it legal in the eyes of the state while the ceremony at the church would be before God and family. The wedding party would consist of the *padrino* for me—my father and then brother when Dad took on his pastoral role. Antonio's mom would stand next to him as the *madrina*. We wouldn't have ring bearers, maids of honor, best men, or attendants. There also wouldn't be presents from a registry. People gave monetary gifts in envelopes at the reception that in theory would cover the costs of the reception with a little extra; there was a small room at the restaurant used for the purpose of opening envelopes in private to pay for the event. The restaurant made the cake.

Most weddings I had attended were simple, church-centered events with receptions following there, so all this sounded expensive and pretentious back then. We tried to relieve my parents' anxiety about the event. Going to Spain was a huge adventure without bringing a wedding into it, but it was important that they would attend.

Antonio had found a bottom-floor flat for us to rent from a member of the church in Alcalá. It had been abandoned for years and needed to be completely repaired and updated. An arrangement was made that all material costs would go toward the rent; Antonio and his father spent every extra hour they had fixing up that place for us. At times I thought I was dreaming.

Back at college for my final semester, I continued to be involved in church, speaking, and taking stats for basketball, and I even had a part in a play. I loved the deep conversations that made me think more profoundly about social issues and the church. The road trips with friends to basketball games and speaking engagements and a couple of trips with my aunt during that time helped take my eyes off myself and see others for good and bad and have meaningful conversations about God and relationships; besides, they were lots of fun. There was one final trip to visit extended family and my prosthetist to say goodbye in Wisconsin.

The daily letters I received from Antonio are still private treasures; we had a countdown to our wedding day. Pablo's and Lynette's little girl was a balm to my soul; I loved the boys dearly, but holding this little one and hearing her coos and soft, sleepy breathing made all life's problems disappear.

I paid even closer attention to Lynette; she was my mentor and my model of a godly wife and mother. Not much older than me, she had a wisdom that was not learned in school. I asked so many questions and exposed my vulnerable heart about my anxiety about marriage and children in particular. Their honesty and love nurtured the wife's and mother's heart in me. I credit them for any confidence I had when I married, and God used their example to encourage me for years.

The days flew by; Lynette and I packed up everything I owned. My classes ended, and my parents arrived. We distributed all my possessions into three categories: going to others, going to Arizona, or going to Spain. My parents had brought my wedding dress, and that was my carry-on. The pile going to Spain consisted of boxes of books that were going book rate via ship, suitcases coming with me, and suitcases coming with Mom, Dad, and Eric when they traveled to Spain. Thankfully, airlines generally allowed two carry-ons and two pieces of checked luggage with generous weight allowances for international travel back in the summer of 1991. I did not hang around for graduation; there were stairs to get up to and down from the stage, and money was needed for things other than a cap and gown. I said my fond farewells through tears; I was so thankful that these goodbyes were almost all "See you soon" in God's family.

My parents dropped me off at O'Hare in Chicago one last time with a thousand details and last-minute instructions and assurances. They drove away with my car and the van while I flew toward my future.

Antonio and I were married in June surrounded by family and friends. And we lived happily ever after.

CHAPTER 10

Faith, Hope, and Love

Well, sort of happily ever after. Antonio and I are flawed you see. His expectations, opinions, needs, and reactions are not the same as mine and vice-versa. Guess what that is? Normal! Yes, there have been blowups due to his hot-blooded Latin ways, and I have given him the silent treatment of cold anger from my stoic Midwestern upbringing. Two very different people became one in the eyes of God and took vows that mean love is a choice to commit and not a warm, fuzzy feeling.

Our advantage was that we had both submitted to God through an extremely difficult time and chosen to trust and obey Him not perfectly but continually. That obedience has a lot to do with how we have loved, fought, and lived. Antonio's love for me reminds me of how Jesus loves me—unconditionally. I am blessed with a man who loves God and therefore can love and accept me.

Life is hard; I don't care who you are. In many ways, being a Christ follower makes life harder, not easier, but in the same breath, it makes it more bearable. My being a Christian requires me to forget myself and find my identity in Christ. I have to hold my feelings up to the light of the Bible and prayerfully consider the right action. That's hard. To be a disciple requires discipline, and I confess that I don't do that well or even like it a lot of times. I would prefer to wallow in my negative emotions and circumstances. Sometimes,

I just want to quit; I don't want to follow anymore because I *feel* it would be easier to follow my heart and impulses, but I just get myself into a world of hurt. That tends to happen when I believe the lies that make me identify more with this world of hurt where I live at this moment than with the One who would pull me out of the filth and "lead me to the Rock that is higher than I" (Psalm 61:2 NIV). Higher than I, yes. "Follow your heart" is a popular saying; I understand what it means, but the problem is that many times, I can't trust my heart. Only when my heart is right with God and is submitted to His Word in obedience does any good come out of following my heart. It's always best to follow the good Shepherd.

Psalm 23, John 10, and so many other passages of scripture talk about the Lord and specifically Jesus as the Shepherd and His people as the sheep—fuzzy, filthy, silly sheep. Their safety is in the flock near the shepherd. They will eat their food source down to the roots and kill it off. They can be standing next to a river and die of thirst. They cannot see or run well. Neither their teeth nor their hooves offer any offensive or defensive advantage. If they try to stand up for themselves against lions and wolves, they end up dead. I don't like the comparison of sheep and myself, but the evidence of my behavior parallels the metaphor. I prefer this.

Invictus

Out of the night that covers me,
Black as the pit from pole to pole,
I thank whatever gods may be
For my unconquerable soul.

In the fell clutch of circumstance
I have not winced nor cried aloud.
Under the bludgeonings of chance
My head is bloody, but unbowed.

Beyond this place of wrath and tears
Looms but the Horror of the shade,
And yet the menace of the years
Finds and shall find me unafraid.

It matters not how strait the gate,
How charged with punishments the scroll,
I am the master of my fate,
I am the captain of my soul.

William Henley wrote this poem in 1875 at age twenty-six after the amputation of one leg and as he was recovering from surgeries to avoid the amputation of the other due to complications with tuberculosis. He was hospitalized and in isolation for nearly three years. He died in 1903. His poem, which was given a title by an editor, has been used many times over and was in keeping with the Victorian British sentiment of keeping a stiff upper lip.[15]

His poem resonates with the rugged American independent spirit and with my misplaced ideals of chance, being in control, independence, death, and resilience. It is true that I can choose what I will do with the circumstances I have been given. In stanza 3, he shakes his fist at death and in stanza 4 at God when alluding to Matthew 7:13–14. After the euphoria wears off the defiant self-determination in the face of suffering, the question has to be asked— To what point and purpose?

This obsession with self—"I am the master of my fate, the captain of my soul"—has led to innumerable shipwrecks of humanity. Many books have been written on the topic of our modern culture, and I leave it to their authors to expound on that, but I bring it up to point out the fallacy of the sentiment in my and so many others' lives. Again, it is my choice what to do with the life I have been given, but I will diverge from popular opinion at this point. We are not masters, but we can choose which master we will serve. I am not a captain, but I do have the choice to make my captain the wind and the waves or the One who commands them.

While I was writing this book, my son married his high school sweetheart at age twenty-one, my age when Antonio and I married. My daughter struggles with questions of faith, direction, and purpose at age nineteen, the same age I was when I was struggling differently and yet the same.

Time has given me a greater perspective. It all feels like a lifetime ago, and yet I have been affected as though it happened yesterday. Antonio and I have already celebrated more than thirty years together on two continents, in two countries, two languages and cultures, over twenty transatlantic flights, four wheelchairs, six sets of legs, four more operations, hospitals, visits to doctors, blood draws, medications, and ointments. It's been fourteen years of teaching English, Spanish, and English as a foreign and second language and then not being able to work because of disability complications. It's been five homes, six churches, family and friends, two kids—private school, public school, home school, university, soccer, swimming, fish, chickens, two rats, three dogs, and one cat.

Our family in 2013

How many experiences can a person have in one lifetime? How many tears and sleepless nights? How much laughter and food shared around a table? How many cups of coffee and conversations with friends? Time and experience have burst the haughty confidence I had in my youth. I find I know much less than I knew at age twenty-five about politics, education, marriage, and raising kids, and yet I understand more profoundly because I have lived so much more. At this point, I have lived many more years without my legs than with them. My convictions about a God in heaven and my complete confidence in His Word, which at many points in this story hung by a thread of faith, have become unshakable. No, I do not have all the answers and cannot explain why God does what He does, but I can tell you about who He is. Sometimes, I will sing joyfully while dancing in my kitchen (moving in a scary, awkward way is what my kids would say), and other times, I will be on my knees with forehead on the floor sobbing and pouring my heart out to God. Being a Christian has not given me an easier life, but it has given me a purposeful one.

God's Word tells me that life is not chaotic and pointless. He is the God of design and purpose throughout time, which He created. This message is made clear from Genesis to Revelation. Greater minds have written much on this purposeful life using the Bible as their starting and ending points, and I defer to them. I have been influenced by Matthew Henry, C. S. Lewis, Chuck Colson, Francis Schaeffer, Norman Geisler, Philip Yancey, Alistair Begg ... There are many others. But without question, the inspired apologetics of the apostle Paul have had the greatest influence on me. Perhaps of all the authors inspired by God to form what today we call our Holy Bible, Paul is the one who most changed my perceptions over the years. His tone has changed. When I was younger, I heard a lecture, but now I hear him as a loving shepherd and pastor pleading with his readers to understand the big picture from the Old Testament to the coming of Jesus Christ, our Lord and Savior.

People talk about having a life verse, but I sort of have a life chapter. Dear Reader, it has taken me decades to really hear and understand what I know now. My prayer is that you will see yourself here also. I find my life's purpose in 2 Corinthians 4. If I have a testimony to share after all these years, it is found there. Whenever I see or hear 2 Corinthians 4, my heart beats a little faster as if I've received word from an old friend.

I understand that this was Paul writing a second letter to the Corinthian church. He was talking about Timothy's and his calling and experiences, but I have found comfort and the purpose for my life reflected here. I believe our lives are to be reflected here as well based on many other passages of scripture, which I'll try to explain.

In 2 Corinthians 4:1 (NIV), the first word is *therefore,* which means I have to back up to figure out what is going on. Chapter 3 talks about the law and Moses in the Old Testament. After being in the presence of God, Moses's face would radiate God's glory in a physical way that made people nervous, so they made him put a veil over his face until he returned to normal. Paul discussed how the law given to Moses in the Old Testament condemned us or in other words led to death because we were incapable of following it perfectly. He told us that from Moses's time to today, a veil is still over our hearts so that we don't understand and can't see unless Jesus takes the veil away.

> But whenever anyone turns to the Lord, the veil is taken away. Now the Lord is the Spirit, and where the Spirit of the Lord is, there is freedom. And we all who with unveiled faces contemplate {reflect} the Lord's glory, are being transformed into his image with ever-increasing glory, which comes from the Lord, who is the Spirit. (2 Corinthians 3:16–18 NIV)

This is the beginning of anyone's testimony of faith. The veil is lifted, and now we see. We hear echoes of these verses in "Amazing Grace."

> Amazing grace! How sweet the sound
> That saved a wretch like me!
> I once was lost, but now am found;
> Was blind, but now I see.

There I was—a wretch, a narcissist, an addict, a religious person, a good person, a bad person, a whatever kind of person but a sinner for sure and thus a lost and blind person. Then 2 Corinthians 3:16 happens, and I can see.

> 'Twas grace that taught my heart to fear,
> And grace my fears relieved;
> How precious did that grace appear
> The hour I first believed.

John Newton wrote these lyrics in 1772, and he understood this apparent contradiction better than most.[16] This foul-mouthed, offensive slave trader was condemned by God's law. He could not find any better word than *wretch* to describe himself in his hymn. He had lived most of his life not caring about what was right or wrong; he was just out to make money. But when he saw the Lord honestly and clearly, for the first time, he was overwhelmed by how filthy and unworthy he was as he stood to be judged before a holy God, and his heart feared. He said it was grace, a better relative of mercy, that taught his arrogant heart to fear.

If I find myself believing that I am a comparatively good religious person, I need to ask God to unveil my eyes so I can experience holy fear because we all stand before God (John 3:16–21, 9:39–41). The ground is level at the foot of the cross. We all stand in the need of grace, amazing grace.

In the next line, Newton penned that the same grace that taught his heart to fear was then relieving that fear.

> Therefore, there is now no condemnation for those who are in Christ Jesus, because through Christ Jesus the law of the Spirit who gives life has set you free from the law of sin and death. (Romans 8:1–2 NIV)

This is where verse 17 of 2 Corinthians 3 comes in too. We have been set free from the law that condemns us that was written by Moses by the same God, but now, salvation comes through Jesus Christ the Lord and has set us free from our condemnation. Newton wrote about how precious this grace was; it was a one-two punch that took his breath away both times.

When we take communion in church, it is to remember Christ's body broken for us and His blood shed for us on the cross, for me, for my sins of arrogance, pride, ego, and selfishness and for my indulgences—"I want what I want"—in my reputation and opinions, placed on Jesus Christ on the cross. I am free because Jesus was condemned in my place. Those who have been saved by Jesus take communion to remember Him with deep gratitude. Then comes verse 18, which tells us that those who have truly seen will never be the same. The Lord begins transforming us to become more like Him.

"Therefore" since we have been saved by His amazing grace and are being transformed into His image through the work of the Holy Spirit, we should increasingly reflect Jesus in our lives—grow and glow. This is where a life of purpose begins; if I don't get this right, nothing else will ultimately matter. This is my life chapter. "Therefore, having this ministry by the mercy of God, we do not lose heart" (2 Corinthians 4:1 NIV).

Automatically, I am enrolled in ministry. In our Western culture, we like to think of ministry as paid positions in the church, but that is wrong. In every book in the New Testament, we repeatedly see that if we have received grace, it is then our ministry to extend grace to others through letting them know about God's grace in our words and actions. This requires the same attitude as Christ; He prayed a lot on earth because life was and is hard. He "put on flesh" and "dwelt among us" (John 1:14 NIV). He lived here, and let's face it—living can be difficult and people can be cruel. Paul reminded us and himself that we should not lose heart.

> Rather, we have renounced secret and shameful ways; we do not use deception, nor do we distort the word of God. On the contrary, by setting forth the truth plainly we commend ourselves to everyone's conscience in the sight of God. (2 Corinthians 4:2 NIV)

I have to renounce being manipulative to promote myself or be successful. I have to speak and live transparently and with integrity before God and humanity. My father and our family were often criticized in the church when I was a teenager because of something that had been said or done. When I was a teenager, I believed in God. Going to the movies was frowned upon by many members of our small congregation. I was allowed to go to the movies, but one time, I felt a little uneasy about the movie my friends wanted to see. I asked my dad for permission to go, and he asked me, "Can you watch this movie with a clear conscience before God? It's not important what I approve or don't approve of, but consider instead what God would approve of. Then you have nothing to be ashamed of in or outside the church." I do everything in God's sight. I can live sincerely before everyone when I am doing right and humbly admit when I am doing wrong. If I compromise this part, my ministry, my life is inauthentic and I become a hypocrite. I have understood this from my teen years on.

Understanding is one thing. Acting on one's understanding

is another. I have faced discouragement because so many friends, coworkers, and classmates did not believe me when I shared my faith. Second Corinthians 4:3–4 (NIV) addresses this unbelief.

> And even if our gospel is veiled, it is veiled to those who are perishing. The god of this age has blinded the minds of unbelievers, so that they cannot see the light of the gospel that displays the glory of Christ, who is the image of God.

This part has taken me longer to understand. I had wanted to believe that if I did everything right, everything would work out right. I knew what the words said that people don't believe; they can't see because their spiritual eyes have been blinded by Satan. Even though I now read this and see so clearly that it is the Lord who takes away the veil, I acted like that was my job, and the problem was that I was never good enough to please everybody in or outside church. There were a few seasons in my life when I tried to quit, resign from ministry if you will. That never did and never will work out because I still wanted to be close to God; I just wanted out of the ministry. But the Spirit of truth is in me, and there is no running or hiding from what He has asked me to do. Like Jonah, we can try, but God has a way of bringing us back. It can get messy. Like Moses, I have eloquently argued with God using my excuses to let me sit out the ministry part, but that's impossible if I am being transformed to be more like Jesus.

> For what we preach is not ourselves, but Jesus Christ as Lord, and ourselves as your servants for Jesus' sake. For God, who said, "Let light shine out of darkness," made his light shine in our hearts to give us the light of the knowledge of God's glory displayed in the face of Christ. (2 Corinthians 4:5–6 NIV)

God had made His light shine in my heart, and in that light, I have known Jesus Christ as my Lord and Savior. That light must continue to shine out of me as I am transformed by degrees to be more and more like Him. Nothing is about me. My identity is found in Christ, which is why I am called a Christian, a term that meant belonging to Christ that was used to describe followers of the Way or disciples in Acts 11:26 (NIV), "The disciples were called Christians first at Antioch." Time and again, I have been humbled in Christ's presence and reminded of my ministry.

I wrote this book for several reasons, but one reason I had not begun it earlier than I did was because I did not feel I reflected His life well enough—as though I first needed to measure up to some imaginary standard before continuing with such a public testimony. My focus was so wrong. Again, nothing is about me. I am accountable for my faith and obedience, but God is the ultimate judge of my life. We are told to trust and to do what He asks of us in His Word and by His Spirit. I believed the lie that I would never be good enough, which is a half-truth from the pit of hell.

God does not grade by comparison like a teacher grading on a curve; He does hold us to a standard, one that we all fail miserably to attain. Romans 3:23 (NIV) reads, "For all have sinned and *fall short* of the glory of God" (emphasis mine). Through Jesus Christ, we have "the light of the knowledge of the glory of God." The only righteous thing about me is Jesus. Period. I will never be good enough; I simply stand in Christ's righteousness that in His grace has been passed on to me.

> For it is by grace you have been saved, through faith—and this is not from yourselves, it is the gift of God—not by works, so that no one can boast. For we are God's handiwork, created in Christ Jesus to do good works, which God prepared in advance for us to do. (Ephesians 2:8–10 NIV)

The only good I do is the good I do through God, who prepared it for me to do through His Son. He knows I can't. Psalm 103:14 (NIV) says, "He knows how we are formed, He remembers that we are dust." Paul understood the contradiction as well. We, the dusty, hold the divine. God chooses to work through us, which is logically inconceivable. It is again a matter of faith, a question of trust that I allowed Satan to infuse doubt into me so that I would not fulfill my purpose. I am still learning to trust God and take Him at His Word. In 2 Corinthians 5, the following chapter, this purpose is clearly defined.

> Therefore, if anyone is in Christ, the new creation
> has come: The old has gone, the new is here! All this
> is from God, who reconciled us to himself through
> Christ and gave us the ministry of reconciliation: that
> God was reconciling the world to himself in Christ,
> not counting people's sins against them. And he has
> committed to us the message of reconciliation. We
> are therefore Christ's ambassadors, as though God
> were making his appeal through us. We implore
> you on Christ's behalf: Be reconciled to God. God
> made him who had no sin to be sin for us, so that
> in him we might become the righteousness of God.
> (2 Corinthians 5:17–21 NIV)

In this body, in Jesus Christ, I have become a new creation because in Jesus I can become the righteousness of God. Jesus paid my debt, so now, God does not count my sin, my failings against me and I am free and able to pursue doing what is right because I am counted as right before God because of Jesus. It makes my head hurt if I think about it and try to figure it all out. How or why can I be loved and accepted by God and be given a responsibility, be entrusted with a message from God to the people around me? The message is clear; our purpose is clear. As Christ followers, we are His ambassadors, His representatives. I am in ministry not because of me but because of who is in me: "But we have this treasure in jars of clay to show that this all-surpassing power is from God and not from us" (2 Corinthians 4:7 NIV).

I am a jar of clay, a broken jar of clay, but I have a treasure in me. Because of Jesus, I have the Holy Spirit in me, and He fills in all my broken places and what's missing in me. I do not have my act together; the Holy Spirit works despite my failings and holds me together and enables me to fulfill my purpose. I just need to be willing.

As children, we used to sing the chorus to "This Little Light of Mine" with our index fingers pointing up. The light is not my light, it's God's light, His Spirit in me. One Sunday morning when I was in my thirties and in the routine of life, the Lord spoke to me in church. I knew as sure as I knew my name what He was telling my heart and mind in my heart and mind. He used that song.

This Little Light of Mine
This little light of mine,
I'm gonna let it shine
This little light of mine,
I'm gonna let it shine
This little light of mine,
I'm gonna let it shine
Let it shine,
Let it shine,
Let it shine.

Hide it under a bushel? No!
I'm gonna let it shine
Hide it under a bushel? No!
I'm gonna let it shine
Hide it under a bushel? No!

I'm gonna let it shine
Let it shine,
Let it shine,
Let it shine.

Jesus said in Matthew 5:15 (NIV), "Nor do people light a lamp and put it under a basket, but on a stand, and it gives light to all in the house." I had tried to be normal for so long and to not stand out in a crowd. I was a wife, a mother, a high school teacher, daughter, sister, and friend. My life was normal. In church that morning, after I had been blessed after a couple shared their testimony of God's faithfulness, God impressed on my heart and mind that I had hidden my light under a bushel of my normality.

Many of my coworkers and acquaintances had no idea how physically challenged I was because I downplayed it as much as possible. However, as a result, I also silenced a large part of my life that demonstrated God's faithfulness to me. All they saw was that I was friendly, competent, hard working, and dependable. I think that most people including my students who knew me knew I was a Christian. It wasn't that I didn't have a testimony for Christ; it was that I wasn't giving Him glory to those around me by using the testimony God had given me. I found myself encouraged when others talked openly about how God had been faithful through financial, family, and physical problems, and yet there I sat silently. I had prayed and been active in church but more as a spectator who avoided drawing attention to myself. I confessed this to our pastor at the next Wednesday evening Bible study, and he encouraged me to write out my testimony. Before long, I found myself again giving public testimony to God's work in my life.

A couple of years after that, my normal changed again. I had to go out on disability again after having been a high school teacher for fourteen years in Spain and Arizona. I felt losses of my identity, my income, my normal, my purpose. It all felt familiar; I'd been there before. This body had carried two babies to term, kept up with them, and worked full time. My body just wouldn't be pushed anymore. I was plagued by inexplicable pain and fatigue. No matter what I did, I couldn't (and still can't) shake it. I went from doctor visits to labs and various procedures feeling as if someone had slapped a sticker on my forehead that read "Please, tell me all your problems." I tried to avoid people in waiting rooms; I was a pro at that normally, but God had different ideas. I met so many people with so much despair and emotional and physical pain that it jarred me awake to a reality I hadn't expected from what I considered normal people. When I would give them a two-minute recap of my story, I would watch their eyes widen; some would tear up, and I tried to encourage them. Some believed in God and some didn't, but I was surprised how often people would tell me that I must have been alive for a purpose and that I should write a book.

I was depressed and frustrated by what was happening to me, but I realized that I was nonetheless leaking out hope and encouragement to people. I was bewildered, disappointed, and in pain, but God kept opening my eyes to two truths—that despite my circumstances, I was blessed beyond measure and that normal people desperately needed Jesus. I knew that, but it became a realization, a much deeper knowing. Though I was feeling down and negative, those were surface feelings under which were love, peace, hope, and faith. I had become so accustomed to having those that I had forgotten how precious they were. It was as if my eyes were opened to see that these things were missing in many of the people around me. Those whose lives were all about the surface had nothing to hold them steady when circumstances spun them out of control.

I knew who was in control. I knew who held me. Neither head knowledge nor intellect allowed me to grasp that, but an understanding that combined the knowledge with the experience that comes when our faith is tested. I was not in the same place that I had been twenty-some years before; my faith was stronger, but was being put to the test again.

But we have this treasure in jars of clay to show
that this all-surpassing power is from God and not
from us. We are hard pressed on every side, but not
crushed; perplexed, but not in despair; persecuted,
but not abandoned; struck down, but not destroyed.
We always carry around in our body the death of
Jesus, so that the life of Jesus may also be revealed
in our body. For we who are alive are always being
given over to death for Jesus' sake, so that his
life may also be revealed in our mortal body. (2
Corinthians 4:7–11 NIV)

I am not better or stronger than anyone else. It is simply this:
"Christ in you, the hope of glory" (Colossians 1:27 NIV). Life as
we know it in these jars of clay is hard. Dying is not hard; it is the
process of dying that takes courage and that begins exactly at the
same moment we are alive. "What is the meaning of life?" is one of
the great questions people of all generations have faced. Just being
alive does not give us meaning or purpose. "To be or not to be?" To
be what exactly? That is my question. "For to me *to live is Christ*, and
to die is gain" (Philippians 1:21 NIV). Paul understood that true
life was Christ, and he wrote this for us. In Romans 7:21 (NIV), he
asked, "Who will deliver me from this body of death?" Exactly right.
Most people in their teens and twenties can easily be persuaded
that their bodies are vessels of life, but with few exceptions, those
in their seventies and older and many before they reach that age
realize that their bodies are vessels of death. The mortality rate is
still 100 percent. This comes as a surprise to so many people; though
intellectually we know the truth, we can find it difficult to accept.

Ecclesiastes 3:11 (NIV) says, "He has also set eternity in the
human heart," and I think that is why we have so much difficulty
growing old; we don't feel different in our essence, soul, and spirit.
Paul understood. We know he had a "thorn in the flesh" that kept
him humble and dependent on God. While it gave him more

spiritual clarity, it made his physical life more difficult. Paul had no fear of death; that would have been a win for him. He believed in the resurrection of the dead and that he would be "with Christ" (Philippians 1:23 NIV) if he died. If, however, God allowed him to continue, then it was for Christ that he lived. Paul saw both as deliverance. To live, to be, has meaning only in God through Jesus Christ.

> So then, death is at work in us, but life is at work in you. It is written: "I believed; therefore I have spoken." Since we have that same spirit of faith, we also believe and therefore speak, because we know that the one who raised the Lord Jesus from the dead will also raise us with Jesus and present us with you to himself. All this is for your benefit, so that the grace that is reaching more and more people may cause thanksgiving to overflow to the glory of God. (2 Corinthians 4:12–15 NIV)

Jim Elliot wrote, "He is no fool who gives what he cannot keep to gain what he cannot lose."[17] I knew what it was to hold on to grief and resentment. I also knew what it was to give it completely to God. I faced whether I would hold on to the pride of my identity that gave me a position in this world or my identity in Christ and my position in heaven.

Jim Elliot was killed on the mission field seven years after writing the quote above; he gave his life for the gospel. His wife and child were asked to give him up to God to continue the good works God had prepared for them. Each of us in our relationship with our Lord is asked to give in a profound way. In a sense, it is an echo of King David's words in the Old Testament concerning not offering a sacrifice to God "that costs me nothing" (1 Chronicles 21:23–25 NIV). If my broken body helps me point others to the faith, love, hope, and peace found in Jesus, that is life. Praise God!

So, if I sincerely believe what the Bible says, I have to speak it, give testimony to it because I believe that this is just the beginning of life. I will be alive again in Jesus's presence in heaven hopefully with all of you! I love you as Jesus loves you. I want you to find real life and experience God's grace because that is His desire.

There have been a few times when God has given me a window to see how He used my flawed self by His powerful Holy Spirit to transform a person from darkness to light, from despair to hope and joy, and from death to life. I have bawled like a baby in amazement and humility and been overwhelmed by gratitude. Being around people who have that living, grateful faith is like no other experience; it's a small taste of what heaven will be like.

God is glorified when sincere hearts praise Him. "He brings us with you into His presence" (2 Corinthians 4:14 ESV). There is nothing more freeing than to be with people who understand God's grace; they extend His grace rather than condemning or trying to fix you. They stand beside you as fellow receivers of grace and share compassion, forgiveness, encouragement, prayer, and thanks with you; it is healing, and it is contagious.

I am blessed to be a part of a women's group that is full of grace. We called ourselves Sisters Loved by God inspired by Beth Moore's *Children of the Day* Thessalonians study. We are spiritual sisters bought and brought together by the blood of Jesus, and because of Him, we are all loved by God. In that grace-filled environment, my spiritual life deepened as I found healing from strongholds of failure, clarity of my purpose, and encouragement to live it and write it out. I have been encouraged and in turn have been able to encourage others. In our group, we have witnessed that grace, God's grace, extended to more people, and that has increased our thanksgiving to God. His Word tells us that He is glorified by that.

"So we do not lose heart." Verse 16 repeats that phrase first stated in verse 1, and I'm so glad because even with all the blessings, I find myself so easily distracted and discouraged. We all need to hear this, but it is repeated twice in this chapter. Bad news, painful days, another heartbreaking story, destruction, and death surround us. We are overwhelmed with information in the twenty-first century, and the majority of it is discouraging and relentless. In John 10:10 (NIV), Jesus said, "The thief comes only to steal and kill and destroy; I have come that they may have life and have it to the full." Satan, the thief, is about his business in this world in the time he has left. No one has been untouched by the evil of sin—theirs or others. Jesus was describing Himself as the good Shepherd who gave abundant life. Paul reminded us again, "So we do not lose heart." These verses are been life giving in purpose and encouragement.

> Therefore we do not lose heart. Though outwardly we are wasting away, yet inwardly we are being renewed day by day. For our light and momentary troubles are achieving for us an eternal glory that far outweighs them all. So we fix our eyes not on what is seen, but on what is unseen, since what is seen is temporary, but what is unseen is eternal. (2 Corinthians 4:16–18 NIV)

My outer self, this body of mine, has definitely seen better days, but my inner self is better than ever.

> Therefore, I urge you, brothers and sisters, in view of God's mercy, to offer your bodies as a living sacrifice, holy and pleasing to God—this is your true and proper worship. Do not conform to the pattern of this world, but be transformed by the renewing of your mind. Then you will be able to test and approve what God's will is—his good, pleasing and perfect will. (Romans 12:1–2 NIV)

The renewal is not automatic; it is intentional.

> Therefore, since we are surrounded by such a great cloud of witnesses, let us throw off everything that hinders and the sin that so easily entangles. And let us run with perseverance the race marked out for us, fixing our eyes on Jesus, the pioneer and perfecter of faith. For the joy set before him he endured the cross, scorning its shame, and sat down at the right hand of the throne of God. (Hebrews 12:1–2 NIV)

I have been transformed; I am not the same person I used to be. The Holy Spirit has transformed me as He has convicted me of sin and convinced me of the truth of the Bible. He still does, and so I am renewed daily.

This life is full of trouble and suffering; Jesus told us that that was the way it was here. John 16:33 (NIV) says, "I have told you these things, so that in me you may have peace. In this world you will have trouble. But take heart! I have overcome the world." Paul entreated us to change our perspective on our troubles and suffering by making a statement that at first can seem ridiculously shocking to us: "for this light and momentary affliction." I may at first want to argue with that assessment, but then it hits me with all the force of an electric shock. All my pain is nothing in comparison to what is promised in eternity. If in my lifetime I can look around and compare my suffering to the benefits of having experienced it here and now, what will heaven be like? These verses restart my faltering heart and sync it back up with God's heart for me. I observe how He patiently, zealously, loyally loves people, His loving-kindness, *checed*,[18] over and over from the beginning to the end of the Bible. God has prepared our way and His purposes for each of us that accomplish His purpose. The Bible documents lives of those who chose to follow or reject God's purpose. We have the promise of eternity. Paul holds on to that promise with both hands if you will, and not only Paul; we have the testimony of the disciples, and countless lives throughout time bear witness to their belief that today is not all there is.

I love Paul's description in the next chapter of this body being a tent, a temporary place to live while we're on excursion away from our true home.

> For we know that if the earthly tent we live in is destroyed, we have a building from God, an eternal house in heaven, not built by human hands. Meanwhile we groan, longing to be clothed instead with our heavenly dwelling, because when we are clothed, we will not be found naked. For while we are in this tent, we groan and are burdened, because we do not wish to be unclothed but to be clothed instead with our heavenly dwelling, so that what is mortal may be swallowed up by life.
>
> Now the one who has fashioned us for this very purpose is God, who has given us the Spirit as a deposit, guaranteeing what is to come. Therefore we are always confident and know that as long as we are at home in the body we are away from the Lord. For we live by faith, not by sight. We are confident, I say, and would prefer to be away from the body and at home with the Lord. So we make it our goal to please him, whether we are at home in the body or away from it. For we must all appear before the judgment seat of Christ, so that each of us may receive what is due us for the things done while in the body, whether good or bad. (2 Corinthians 5:1–10 NIV)

Twice in chapter 4, he wrote, "So we do not lose heart" (vv. 1, 16). Twice in chapter 5, he wrote, "We are confident" (vv. 6, 8). We know the end of the story.

One day, I will go home. I know why I'm not comfortable here; this is not my home. I know why I don't fit in; this is not my home. My purpose and priority are not to be influenced by what I see: "We walk by faith, not by sight" (v. 7). All of us who call Jesus Christ our Lord and our God are to focus on the eternal. We live here and now, but when I interact with people and circumstances, I am to have an eternal perspective.

The things I see and experience are temporary, but the unseen is eternal. The inner self, the spirit, the soul, is the part of us that matters most to God. We have been placed in this world in physical bodies in a set of circumstances God knows all about. We have been entrusted with the care of this physical world and our physical bodies with the gifts and limitations God has allowed in our lives. If God has allowed your circumstances, He will be faithful to you in them.

I have been reading the Bible for years and am continually amazed at how the Spirit speaks to me through His Word and gives me an understanding that is not necessarily new but is richer and deeper. He gives love, life, and truth. Dear one, fix your eyes on Jesus. No matter what you are facing, lift your eyes to Him. Take the step of faith to simply come into His presence, wait, and put your hope in Him. "Taste and see that the Lord is good; blessed is the one who takes refuge in him" (Psalm 34:8 NIV).

Satan wants you to question, doubt, fear, and compare; he is also all about instant gratification, as he twists truth and desire into lies that steal, kill, and destroy. Do not give him that foothold. Remember that you are dearly loved by God; take all the weight of your questions, doubts, fears, and discontent into His presence and pour out your heart to Him; He already knows. The Holy Spirit will intercede for you. Stop; be still in His presence, look in the Bible, and listen for His leading. Be persistent. Although there are times of silence, He will reveal Himself in His perfect time. Stay in His Word, the Bible: treasure it, study it, discuss it, write it, and memorize it.

The Word of the Lord endures forever. (1 Peter
1:25 NIV)

All Scripture is God-breathed and is useful for
teaching, rebuking, correcting and training in
righteousness, so that the servant of God may
be thoroughly equipped for every good work. (2
Timothy 3:16-17 NIV)

Your word is a lamp for my feet, a light on my path.
(Psalm 119:105 NIV)

Take the helmet of salvation and the sword of
the Spirit, which is the word of God. (Ephesians
6:17 NIV)

Beloved child of God, I encourage you to "lift your eyes" beyond
this moment and see the God who loves you and invites you to live
this life with your hope set on Jesus having His Spirit now and being
in His presence for all eternity (see 1 Peter 1:3–9). The Lord promises
reward to those who seek Him (Hebrews 11:6). Trust Him! Hold
on to His promises, and in your prayers, speak them to God like
reminders, as is modeled in scripture. He is faithful, and His grace
is enough. Rest in His presence. You are His joy. You are saved by
grace. You will be in heaven with Him. You are loved by God!

To Him who is able to keep you from stumbling
and to present you before his glorious presence
without fault and with great joy—to the only God
our Savior be glory, majesty, power and authority,
through Jesus Christ our Lord, before all ages, now
and forevermore! Amen. (Jude 24–25 NIV)

ENDNOTES

1   A. B. Warner, "Jesus Loves Me; This I Know," 1859.
2   E. Elliot, *Let Me Be a Woman: Notes to My Daughter on the Meaning of Womanhood* (Wheaton, IL: Tyndale House, 1976), 10.
3   CDC, "Meningococcal Disease," retrieved April 6, 2020. https://www.cdc.gov/meningococcal/about/index.html.
4   M. Henry, *Matthew Henry Commentary*, retrieved July 25, 2020, https://classic.biblegateway.com/resources/matthew-henry/Jer.10.17-Jer.10.25.
5   N. Borop and M. Baldwin, "My Soul Desire," recorded by D. Williams, on *So Glad I Know*, 1986.
6   Brumley, "This World Is Not My Home," 1937.
7   C. S. Lewis, *Mere Christianity* (New York: Touchstone, 1996), 176.
8   Chisholm and Runyon, "Great Is Thy Faithfulness," 1923.
9   D. Rambo, "I Go to the Rock," (John T. Benson Publishing Co. /ASCAP (admin. by Brentwood-Benson Music Publishing, Inc., 1977), https://www.thecrabbfamily.com/lyrics/gototherock.html
10 A. B. Warner, "Jesus Loves Me; This I Know."
11 C. N. Wells, "Held," on *Awaken*, recorded by N. Grant, 2005.
12 E. V. Hill, "The Lord Gives and the Lord Takes Away," 1987, https://www.drjamesdobson.org/broadcasts/dr-ev-hill-death-his-wife-1
13 E. Elliot, *Shadow of the Almighty* (Grand Rapids: Zondervan, 1958), 89.
14 E. Elliot, *Shadow of the Almighty*, 94.
15 William Ernest Henley, "Invictus," *Book of Verses,* 1888, retrieved September 4, 2020. https://www.poetryfoundation.org/poets/william-ernest-henley.
16 B. Piper, "Behind the Song: John Newton, 'Amazing Grace,'" retrieved April 5, 2020. https://americansongwriter.com/who-wrote-amazing-grace/.
17 E. Elliot, *Shadow of the Almighty, 108.*
18 BibleHub, "*checed.* Strong's Hebrew Concordance number 2617," retrieved August 8, 2020, https://biblehub.com/str/hebrew/2617.htm.

BIBLIOGRAPHY

BibleHub. "*checed. Strong's Hebrew Concordance* number 2617." Retrieved August 8, 2020. https://biblehub.com/str/hebrew/2617.htm.

Borop, N., and Baldwin, M. "My Soul Desire." *So Glad I Know.* Recorded by D. Williams. 1986.

Brumley, A. E. "This World Is Not My Home." 1937.

CDC. "Meningococcal Disease." Retrieved April 6, 2020. https://www.cdc.gov/meningococcal/about/index.html.

Chisholm, R. O., and Runyon, W. M. "Great Is Thy Faithfulness." 1923.

Elliot, E. *Shadow of the Almighty.* Grand Rapids: Zondervan, 1958.

Elliot, E. *Let Me Be a Woman: Notes to My Daughter on the Meaning of Womanhood.* Wheaton, IL: Tyndale House, 1976.

Henley, William Earnest. "Invictus." *Book of Verses.* 1888. Retrieved September 4, 2020. https://www.poetryfoundation.org/poets/william-ernest-henley.

Henry, M. *Matthew Henry Commentary.* Retrieved July 25, 2020. https://classic.biblegateway.com/resources/matthew-henry/Jer.10.17-Jer.10.25.

Hill, E.V. "The Lord Gives and the Lord Takes Away." 1987. https://www.drjamesdobson.org/broadcasts/dr-ev-hill-death-his-wife-1

Lewis, C. S. *Mere Christianity.* New York: Touchstone, 1996.

Piper, B. "Behind the Song: John Newton, 'Amazing Grace.'" Retrieved April 5, 2020. https://americansongwriter.com/who-wrote-amazing-grace/.

Rambo, D. "I Go to the Rock." John T. Benson Publishing Co. / ASCAP (admin. by Brentwood-Benson Music Publishing, Inc.), 1977. https://www.thecrabbfamily.com/lyrics/gototherock.html

Warner, A. B. "Jesus Loves Me; This I Know." 1859.

Wells, C. N. "Held." *Awaken.* Recorded by N. Grant. 2005.

Printed in the United States
by Baker & Taylor Publisher Services